Fireside Chats to Fire Up Churches

Michael A. Cramer

Published for the Power for Living Ministry, Inc.

Produced by JM Press, Inc. Brentwood, TN

All Scripture Quotations are taken from the New King James Version of the Holy Bible.

ISBN: 0-9717532-4-5

First Printing

PRINTED IN THE UNITED STATES OF AMERICA

DEDICATION

I dedicate this book to my beautiful wife, Cindi. Her quiet strength and gentle spirit enriches my life, and enhances our ministry. Cindi is the love of my life, my best friend, and my greatest encourager. I thank God for her loving and faithful support. I also dedicate this book to my late brother, Dennis L. Cramer. His unwavering confidence in my leadership was a tremendous blessing and a tribute to our bond of brothers. God used the final months of Denny's life to profoundly affirm the call of God on my life.

ENDORSEMENTS

"Mike Cramer has provided 'a super-charged vitamin pill' that every congregation and pastor should read and absorb! This veteran pastor uses a positive approach to share his wisdom, which makes the reading inspirational. There is gold in those pages! Don't miss it!!"—*David Wheeler, Professor of Evangelism, Liberty University and LBTS.*

"Every pastor and church leader needs to get his hands on *Fireside Chats to Fire Up Churches!* When I started reading it, I could not put it down. Mike's motivational style challenges me to 'pick up my game' and conquer another mountain. This book is a grand slam!"—*Dave Engbrecht, Senior Pastor, Nappanee Missionary Church, Nappanee, IN.*

"Mike Cramer draws from over 25 years of pastoral ministry to simply, yet powerfully, motivate church leaders to rethink what they do, in light of the Gospel. Each compelling chapter captivates you for the next; making the book an easy read that is difficult to put down."—*Tim Goble, Senior Pastor, Grace Evangelical Free Church, Colville, WA.*

"Mike Cramer offers extremely helpful advice to revitalize a church. A young pastor starting out, or a veteran pastor who has hit the wall, will be encouraged and challenged. Read and act!" —*Alvin Reid, Professor of Evangelism, Southeastern Baptist Theological Seminary.*

"Excellent! Great Insights! Mike Cramer has a very fluid style, which makes the book enjoyable. A great read...Pastors will love it!"—*Scott Camp, Senior Pastor, Fellowship of Joy, Grand Prairie, TX.*

"Mike Cramer provides the best of his experience and wisdom distilled into 20 shot-in-the-arm chapters. This book touches all the bases that every leader faces. Read to grow and pass along some copies to your friends. They will thank you many times over!" —*Scott Nichols, Senior Pastor, Crossroads Community Church, Carol Stream, IL.*

"With humor, candor, and refreshing optimism, this seasoned pastor opens his play book to reveal invaluable principles that any leader can benefit from and apply."—*Darin V. Garton, Pastor, Oak Creek Community Church, Mishawaka, IN.*

"Mike Cramer challenges you to think and plan creatively without compromising the preaching of the life-changing power of the gospel. Pull up a chair. You don't want to miss these fireside chats!"—*Morris H. Chapman, President Emeritus, Executive Committee, SBC.*

"Mike Cramer is truly one who has 'stuck it out' and 'stayed by the stuff' in ministry. You are given a front row seat to both the trials and victories of this seasoned Pastor. Get ready to be encouraged and inspired."—*Joe Thomas, Dean of Students, Criswell College.*

"This book is an important 'manual' to guide those truly interested in seeing their church thrive. Read it. Digest it. Let the Holy Spirit make the adjustments necessary in your life and church." —*Stephen P. Davis, Vice President, Midwest Region NAMB, SBC.*

"Mike Cramer offers proven ways to move your church outside the walls of isolation to engage the lost world with the Light of the Gospel. The reader will sense the burning fires of renewal for his own ministry."—*John Rogers, Evangelism Team Leader, SCBI.*

"Hearing the wise-witness and insightful words of a veteran pastor will reassure and refresh weary warriors."—*Bud Hopkins, Dean & Professor Emeritus, Moody Theological Seminary.*

"One does not have to agree with every proposal in order to profit profoundly from *Fireside Chats to Fire Up Churches*. Here is a pastor who has been incredibly used by God in what would usually be considered a difficult assignment. This will encourage your heart and challenge your perspective."—*Paige Patterson, President, Southwestern Baptist Theological Seminary.*

"With encouraging stories from his own experiences, Mike Cramer provides many practical ideas for those longing to impact their community for Christ. You will lose sleep reading. You will lose sleep dreaming. You will lose sleep implementing. You will die tired...but satisfied!"—*Tom Davis, Academic Dean, Word of Life Bible Institute.*

"This is an excellent book that is practical, positive and powerful. Mike Cramer not only has a vision to reach the lost, but also details a variety of ventures used to accomplish it. I highly recommend it!"—*Wendell Calder, Evangelist, Local Church Evangelism.*

CONTENTS

INTRODUCTION

In January of 1985, I stopped my car, and dusted the snow off the sign of a little Baptist Church in Mishawaka, Indiana. I noticed there was a place on the sign for the name of the pastor, but none was listed. The church building and property appeared to be vacant. However, after doing some research, I discovered that the church was actually in existence. Therefore, I contacted the chairman of the deacons and offered to preach their Sunday services.

In February of 1985, I preached my first sermon at that little Baptist Church. There were only 23 in attendance that Sunday, including my wife and me, and our two preschool children at the time. Interestingly enough, the members in attendance were all southern transplants from Alabama, Mississippi, and Tennessee.

Soon I faced a decision as a twenty-six year old young man. On one hand, I was asked to candidate for a youth pastor position at a large church in the south, where my friend served as the senior pastor. The "game plan" included attending New Orleans Seminary during the week, and serving as youth pastor on the weekends. This sounded like a great opportunity, and we gave it prayerful consideration.

On the other hand, I was asked to serve as pastor at the little Baptist Church in Indiana. The church was located just a few miles from Notre Dame University, and seemed to offer some potential for growth. However, the congregation had never really connected with the Catholic community. Therefore, my wife and I prayerfully sought the Lord's will, and God clearly directed us to serve Him in Mishawaka, Indiana.

Now, the once little Baptist Church has transitioned into: New Life, Home of Positive Faith. Today, several hundred attend weekly, and many of them have come to faith in Christ through our positive faith ministry. Special sevices have exceeded fifteen hundred in attendance, and our outdoor Freedom Festival has drawn crowds up to five thousand. Our multi-staff leadership has also been developed from within our own congregation. This helps us to better identify with our community, and increases our influence for Christ.

The purpose of this book is to provide helpful insight for churches to be more   effective in ministry. This is a book of principles, not a "how to" book on church growth. New Life has adjusted a few methods along the way, but we hold firm to the mission of the Great Commission. We believe in the life-changing power of the gospel, and we are confident in the timeless truth of scripture. We are committed to the principles of planting, and watering the seed of the gospel, as we trust God for the harvest.

My goal is for God to use *Fireside Chats to Fire Up Churches* for His glory. I pray that dedicated pastors and faithful church leaders will be encouraged in ministry. I believe this book can help you "dust the snow off your sign" and take a fresh look at the power of God. I trust that God will bless your life, and fan the flame of inspirational hope in your heart, as you read these Fireside Chats.

CHAPTER 1

BIG DREAMS CAN OVERCOME SMALL MINDS

Dreams inspire hope. Dreams ignite enthusiasm. Dreams increase potential. When a spark falls on a blade of wet grass, nothing happens. When a spark falls on concrete, nothing happens. However, when a spark falls on a powder keg, you get an explosion. Dreams are the powder keg that when united with a spark of enthusiasm will create the explosive power of positive potential.

Martin Luther King Jr. said: "I have a dream" and millions of Americans were inspired with positive hope. The simple phrase: "If you can dream it, you can do it" motivated Walt Disney to build an empire of entertainment around Mickey Mouse. The Apostle Peter had a dream in the tenth chapter of Acts, and the New Testament Church began to "think outside the box" in terms of reaching people for Christ.

Dreams require the kind of faith that is spelled: R-I-S-K. Faith sees the invisible, believes the incredible, and receives the impossible. Faith is also closely related to its partner called vision. Faith is the ability to look at something with vision, and become optimistic about the future. In a similar way, vision is the ability to look at something through the "eyes of faith" as you believe the best is yet to come. Faith and vision will help you see beyond the way *Dreams require the kind of faith that is spelled: R-I-S-K.* something is in the present, to what it can become in the future.

Successful leaders have the ability to translate vision into reality. In fact, the way you transfer an inspirational dream into a realistic goal is by developing a workable plan. However, there is very little inspirational value by initially announcing to the people: "I have a strategic plan." That will come later. The first thing that is required in "raising the mental bar" of the potential for the future, is to develop a dream worth embracing.

Focus on positive promises in the Word of God to increase your faith. Some of my favorite verses for this purpose are: *With God all things are possible* (Matthew 19:26): *If you can believe, all things are possible to him who believes* (Mark 9:23): *For with God nothing will be impossible* (Luke 1:37), and last but not least: *I can do all things through Christ who strengthens me* (Philippians 4:13). Those are just a few of the many positive promises in Scripture that can "light your fire" and expand your vision for the future.

Be sure to keep in mind that we are on the winning team (I Corinthians 15:57). Along with focusing on some positive promises of God's Word, read the many powerful stories concerning the great champions of faith in Scripture. Focus on the fact that we serve the same all-powerful God as they did. This will help give you the courage to look past your current problems, and the confidence to believe in your future potential. It will increase your vision for the church, and help you develop an inspirational dream for reaching your community. It will also help you plan accordingly to experience favor from the Lord.

Remember, it is impossible to pour a gallon of water into an eight-ounce cup. The one container is simply too small. Unfortunately, this seems to be a major problem with far too many ministries. God is ready, willing, and able to pour out His blessing in a big way, but the "container of our minds" is simply too small. It is time to dream big dreams and work with God as we believe that Christ is able to do: *Exceedingly abundantly above all that we ask or think, according to the power that works in us* (Ephesians 3:20). It is just that simple.

In June of 1985, I became the pastor of a small handful of people numbering about twenty-five in attendance. One of the first things I noticed in the early days of our ministry was the defeated mentality of the congregation. I suppose it was understandable to a certain degree because of their past tradition. After all, they had struggled to even keep the doors open for thirty years. Therefore, the idea of actually prospering in ministry was a real stretch for most of the people at that time. Consequently, we had to overcome the tendency to focus on the past tradition, and develop the faith to see the vision of a future hope.

The other glaring reality was the small-minded vision of the church, which was located in a fairly large community. The small church building sat on one acre of land with a grass parking lot. The inside of the building was extremely dated and the carpet was completely worn out. The future plans consisted of: "someday" building a new 200-seat auditorium, converting the existing building into classrooms, and paving the parking lot. This was "their dream" in a town of over forty thousand people, and the greater community at large consisting of more than three hundred thousand people. It was clearly evident that their "container to receive God's potential blessing" was far too small.

We started dreaming a little bigger as we reached people for Christ one at a time. We expanded our vision based on the "peak to peek" principle. In other words, when we would reach one mountain peak, we were able to envision something a little larger as we "peeked" at the next mountain to be scaled. Therefore, we would launch a bigger vision from the new platform for ministry that God had lifted us up to. This concept can be repeated over and over as you "stair-step" your way to greater ministry potential. Currently, New Life is located on fifteen acres of ground with an 862-seat worship stadium, recreational gym, coffee shop, plenty of classrooms, and several hundred people in weekly attendance.

It is important to "walk before you run" in terms of increasing your vision. Basically, allow your dream to unfold in bite size pieces that can be digested. In other words, if you are averaging fifty in Sunday morning worship, it is a little premature to begin talking about the day you will have fifty thousand in worship. However, it is a realistic goal to target one hundred in attendance as you dream together for the upcoming church year.

I also believe very strongly in the collective power of synergy. A team will beat a group of individuals every time. Michael Jordan is considered one of the greatest basketball players of all time, but the Chicago Bulls did not win the championships until Jordan had a great supporting cast. Then they became almost unstoppable.

It is also important to "soar with your strengths" in ministry. Everybody has strengths and weaknesses. Therefore, a team that "plays to their strengths" can reduce the drawbacks of individual weaknesses, and increase the collective productivity. People are fulfilled as they serve in areas of their personal strength, and the body grows in the process.

It also increases the passion in ministry because people are motivated internally. This is so much better than guilt motivation, which is short lived and builds resentment as well. However, when people experience internal motivation, it allows leaders to be encouragers, which creates a positive atmosphere and a contagious attitude.

The natural result of this inspirational environment is an increased creativity for developing new ministry opportunities. This in turn, ignites a fresh spark of enthusiasm, which inspires an even greater vision for influence. It is a cycle of success that increases your influence in the community, and inspires a positive spirit in the church.

In time, as people begin to grasp what can be accomplished by working together, a fresh vision can be cast for the ministry. For us, we eventually developed a new dream for a new day. It was based on the concepts of faith, hope, and love.

Faith ignites true success; Hope inspires true success, and Love increases true success.

We believe that: Faith ignites true success; Hope inspires true success, and Love increases true success.

Therefore, our goal is to influence our culture with positive faith, powerful hope, and the perfect love that is only found in our perfect Savior, the Lord Jesus Christ.

When I think about big dreams overcoming small minds, I am reminded of a story about Harry Houdini. As you know, he was one of the greatest escape artist of all time. In fact, he often boasted that no jail in the world could hold him. Houdini was confident that he could pick any lock, and he repeatedly proved it to crowds all over the world.

On one occasion, as a jailer put Houdini to the test, it looked like Harry would not be able to unlock it. He worked for several hours, but was unsuccessful in his escape attempt. Finally, drenched in sweat and in complete exhaustion, Houdini fell against the bars of the jail cell door. To his astonishment, the door swung wide open. You see the jailer had not locked it! The only place the cell door was locked was in Houdini's mind. Even the great Harry Houdini could not succeed as long as his mind was locked shut.

The same is true for any church that closes its mind to its potential. Too often, the greatest obstacle we face is the one we have created in our mind. That is why it is so important to occasionally take a fresh look through the eye of faith, and develop a new dream for a new day. Refuse to "sell short" the size of container you are designing to receive the blessing of God. Go ahead, "expand your container" and you might increase the amount of God's favor on your ministry.

Sometimes, a simple strategy of counting to ten can make a big dream believable. For example, when you are faced with a challenge, consider writing down ten ways you can overcome the obstacle. This is a practice I have done repeatedly through the years. In the spring of 1999, I decided to apply this principle in a meeting with the deacons. We needed to purchase an additional five acres of ground, at a cost of sixty thousand dollars, in order to expand the ministry.

I suggested to the men that we receive the entire amount in one special offering on a Sunday morning one month from then. I must tell you that they initially looked at me like I was crazy. However, I asked that we at least list ten ways it could be done. I went first and wrote on the board that we could find one "sugar daddy" to donate sixty thousand dollars. This brought a chuckle, but no volunteers!

Then one of the guys stated that we could reverse it, and ask for sixty people to each donate one thousand dollars. Instantly, it started looking more attainable. By the time we had listed ten different ways to achieve the goal, there was literally a "spirit of electricity" as the men bounced around with uncontrollable excitement. We went from complete doubt, to absolute faith in a matter of twenty minutes.

Four weeks later we received the special offering, which totaled over eighty thousand dollars (not pledges, this was actual money in the plate)! The regular offering was also over twenty thousand dollars that day as well. We had not "robbed Peter to pay Paul" as we received over one hundred thousand dollars in one day. This was also at a time when our budget was roughly ten thousand dollars a week. We bought the additional ground with money to spare.

Yes, dreams inspire hope, ignite enthusiasm, and increase potential. Most importantly, big dreams can overcome small minds.

CHAPTER 2

POSITIVE FAITH:
THE BEST WAY TO LIVE

Everybody can choose to be either a balcony dweller or a basement dweller. A balcony dweller lifts people up to a higher level of living. They see the bright side of life, and help others discover the joy as well. The balcony dweller embraces the "Philippians 4:8 principle" of focusing on the positive aspects of faith. Basically, a balcony dweller is someone who sees the glass as half full. Therefore, the balcony dweller is an encouragement to people all around them.

On the other hand, the basement dweller drags people down to a lower level of living. They see the dark side of life as they look at the world from a negative point of view. Basically, the basement dweller sees the glass as half empty. Unfortunately, the basement dweller becomes a discouragement to people they come into contact with in the journey of life.

A balcony dweller lifts people up to a higher level of living.

The scripture says that: *Pleasant words are like a honeycomb, Sweetness to the soul, and health to the bones* (Proverbs 16:24). In other words, we have the ability to inspire others with hope and encouragement. Our words can literally be used of God to boost the spirit of another human being.

The Bible also says that: *Death and life are in the power of the tongue, And those who love it will eat of its fruit* (Proverbs 18:21). Bottom line, there is tremendous power in our words. They can either build people up, or bury them in the ground. The balcony dweller is careful to be a life builder, but the basement dweller is a life destroyer.

Jesus also made it clear that: *Out of the abundance of the heart, the mouth speaks* (Matthew 12:34). Therefore, it could be said that the tongue is like a ladle that simply reveals what is in the pot. The ladle does not prepare the food; it is simply used to serve it. The ladle is dipped into the pot and the food is dished out. The same is true about the tongue; it reaches into our heart, and dishes out what is inside. Therefore, it is crucial that we fill our mind and heart with positive thoughts. This prepares the way for positive words of encouragement to be shared with others.

> *We all have a lens and a filter by which we view and intepret life.*

We all have a lens and a filter by which we view and interpret life. A positive lens will help us look at life in a positive light. A positive filter will also help us interpret life in a positive way. Therefore, the best way to keep a clear lens and a clean filter is by building our lives on the concept of positive faith. It truly helps people "look for the good and find it."

I am also convinced that building a positive faith ministry is a great platform for sharing the good news of God's love. I believe in positive faith. My life verse is Matthew 19:26, which states: *With God all things are possible.* This verse has been foundational in my personal life and in the ministry as well. It has helped us build bridges with the community in many ways, and helps capture a positive attitude at the church as well.

I believe that positive faith is very culturally relevant as well. Today's generation is searching for a faith that offers hope for today. Therefore, a positive approach to biblical Christianity is a great way to reach out with the good news of the gospel. I am convinced that a positive-minded believer will be a magnet for the gospel. People are naturally drawn to a balcony dweller in life that lifts others up to "life on the high road." By the way, people are also turned off by a "basement dweller" that constantly drags others down to the dark side of life. Therefore, positive faith is the best way to travel.

The idea of positive faith is also a "good fit" with our culture that emphasizes a healthy self-esteem. The days of "beating people over the head with the Bible" are over. Our modern culture will "tune out" a negative minded believer in a heartbeat. If our message is perceived as harsh and judgmental, we might as well "save our breath." The lost will not be listening.

It is like a parent that is always shouting at their kids, eventually the children tune out the angry parent as soon as the voice is raised. The same is true with communicating the gospel to our generation. If we want them to listen, it is best to share the good news with a big smile and a loving attitude. By the way, smiling should be a natural expression of good news!

Don't get me wrong; I am not talking about "watering down" the message. I am simply suggesting that we proclaim the good news in a manner that best represents our message. Positive Faith is based on the concept that: *The Bible is not a rulebook to make you miserable; it is a roadmap to make you successful.* Positive faith enables a believer to build a positive attitude for success in life on the foundational substance of the Christian Faith. Knowing that your past is forgiven, and your future is secure, provides the positive motivation and powerful inspiration for a better life in the present. Positive Faith will enrich your own life, and help you become a positive influence for the Christian Faith.

Building a ministry based on Positive Faith will help connect with the culture and will encourage the church as well. We like to quote my positive faith motto which states: *My positive attitude in life is an expression of my positive faith, which embraces the powerful truth that: "with God all things are possible."* This helps create a positive atmosphere and sets an "inspirational tone" for our worship services. In a culture that is looking for a faith that works on Monday morning, I believe a positive approach to biblical Christianity is a great way to accomplish that goal.

The emphasis on positive faith, and the exciting energy level in our Worship service is gradually changing the complexion of our church. The Praise Band, inspirational music, and a motivational message rooted in the Word of God have caused a shift in the type of "positive transfer" we are now attracting. We are drawing some people from "seeker churches" that are looking for the preaching of the Word. They have grown tired of the "cotton candy" teaching in the seeker churches. They have learned that cotton candy is sweet, but you cannot live on it. Therefore, they enjoy our unique blend of contemporary music and expositional preaching.

Positive Faith provides several building blocks for believers. First it helps them see the Bible as their "trail guide" on the path of success. After all, the Bible is not a rulebook to make you miserable; it is a roadmap to make you successful. The Bible itself is very clear that meditating on the Word, and obeying the Word will: *make your way prosperous, and then you will have good success* (Joshua 1:8). Therefore, it is okay for Christians to develop a mindset for true success in life.

Positive Faith also recognizes the value of enthusiasm in life. We are instructed to: *do everything heartily as to the Lord* (Colossians 3:23). The word "heartily" comes from two root words, which give us the word "enthusiasism" today. "En" means "in" and "theos" refers to God. Therefore, enthusiasm is literally the power of God at work in a believer. I believe that enthusiasm is a contagious fire of positive desire because your outlook determines your outcome.

Positive Faith also helps people discover the adversity advantage. We all endure hardships from time-to-time. However, when properly understood, adversity can become your teacher instead of your undertaker. Positive faith helps you apply the "Romans 8:28 principle" of looking for the good and finding it. They learn that every obstacle is an opportunity to learn the character quality of perseverance, which leads to hope (Romans 5:3-4). This helps turn a burden into a blessing because: when there is hope for the future; there is power in the present. Therefore, Positive Faith helps people discover the opportunity behind every obstacle.

Bottom line: Positive Faith helps people keep a positive perspective in life. It reminds people that the sun is shining, even if you cannot see it. I was reminded of that truth while flying from Detroit, Michigan to South Bend, Indiana one cold, cloudy, dark and dismal day in February. The sky was gray as we took off in flight. However, as we rose above the cloud cover; the sun was shining brightly. I thought to myself, the sun had been shining all along, however, I could not see it until we got above the clouds.

The same is true in life. Sometimes things appear worse than they actually are. However, applying a good dose of Positive Faith will help you: *Set your mind on things above, not on things of the earth* (Colossians 3:2). This brings an eternal perspective, and reminds you that the "Son" is still shining brightly on His throne. As a result of your positive perspective on life, you will be able to reach your potential in life.

One final thought on the value of building a positive faith ministry is that it helps people water the seeds of faith, and pour gas on the spark of enthusiasm. It could be said that everyone carries two buckets. Basically, each person carries a bucket of gas and a bucket of water.

As a result of your positive perspective on life, you will be able to reach your potential in life.

Essentially, your influence will be determined by the way you distribute your buckets. Consequently, you must decide if you want to be a positive influence or a negative influence.

For example, the balcony dweller will pour their bucket of gas on the spark of excitement. This will provide an enthusiastic fire of positive energy. This positive person pours their bucket of water on a negative spark. This enables them to put out negative fires before they have a chance to spread their toxic poison. This results in the powerful influence on others from the positive attitude of balcony dwellers in life.

Basement dwellers, on the other hand, have the same two buckets, but they use them very differently. This negative person pours their bucket of gas on the negative spark. They fan the flames of inflammatory talk and destructive energy. They also pour their bucket of water on any spark of excitement they find. Naturally, they kill the enthusiasm of people and create a toxic environment. Their negative influence is discouraging to people and damaging to the work of the ministry.

The Scripture is very clear that God wants us to be positive people of encouragement. In fact, one of the most important reasons we gather for worship is to encourage one another in Christian fellowship. After all, it may only be a short distance between a "pat on the back" and a "kick in the pants," but it can make all the difference in the world! Yes, God is pleased and the ministry is blessed as we give others that "shot in the arm" of encouragement.

There is a great deal of truth in the concept that our attitude determines our altitude in life. Therefore, it is a good idea to build a positive faith ministry of balcony dwellers, instead of a negative minded group of basement dwellers. Since everyone is carrying the same two buckets, we all have the same opportunity to be a positive influence. Just pour your bucket of water on the negative spark and pour your bucket of gas on the spark of excitement. Then, experience the joy of watching it grow into a blazing fire of enthusiasm for the glory of God. I believe you will discover that Positive Faith is truly the best way to live. After all, the view looks so much better from the balcony than it does from the basement. Go ahead and try it; you just might like it!

CHAPTER 3

REVIVING TRUE RELEVANCE

In 1972, a woman from Mishawaka, Indiana, by the name of Dixie went to visit her mother near Lake Tahoe, Nevada. She was traveling down a mountain road on a dark night when a deer leaped in front of her car. She swerved to miss the deer and crashed into the side of the mountain. The impact threw her from the car and she fell into a ditch by the side of road. When she was finally discovered, she was pronounced dead at the scene, and taken to a hospital morgue. An attendant at the morgue pulled a sheet over Dixie's body, and began making some preliminary preparations.

He turned on some background music and began going about his business. Fortunately, he also made a shocking discovery! He looked down and saw Dixie keeping time with the music by tapping her little finger! The doctors were called in and they revived the woman! What everybody thought was dead, was actually alive! Amazingly enough, the only sign of life in her body was the tapping of her finger to some music playing in the background.

In many ways, that incredible story is a sad picture of the modern church, which has been pronounced dead at the scene. A "sheet has been pulled over the Bible" because the Word of God is not considered relevant anymore. Consequently, the church has become lifeless, and has fallen helplessly in a ditch. Only on rare occasions, do we demonstrate any signs of spiritual vitality.

The Apostle Paul gave a passionate plea to a young pastor named Timothy to: *Preach the Word* (II Timothy 4:2). This was the last letter that Paul wrote, and he shared what was closest to his heart. He gave several reasons for us to remain faithful to biblical preaching. First and foremost, the Bible helps people understand their need of salvation through faith in Christ. Paul reminded Timothy of the importance of: *the Holy Scriptures, which are able to make you wise for salvation through faith which is in Christ Jesus* (II Timothy 3:15).

The Bible has been called the "Jesus Book" for obvious reasons. Jesus said that: *the Scriptures testify of Him* (John 5:39). The Old Testament points to Christ coming to the cross. The Gospels reveal that Christ died on the cross and rose again from the dead. The Epistles teach us how to live for Christ, and the Book of Revelation reminds us that we are on the winning team. Anywhere you look in Scripture, you will find Christ on every page of the Bible. That is precisely why the Bible is timeless truth that transcends to every culture of every generation. Trust me, the message of Christ is still very relevant today.

The Bible is timeless truth that transcends to every culture of every generation.

I remember the time a young woman visited our church. We made a follow up visit and shared the plan of salvation with her. She explained that she wanted to believe in Christ, but she had one problem. She told us that she did not believe in the bodily resurrection of Christ. Therefore, I asked her to read the gospel of John over the next few weeks.

After all, the purpose of John's gospel is revealed when it says: *These things are written that you may believe that Jesus is the Christ, the Son of God, and that believing you may have life in His name* (John 20:31). Three weeks later, her doubt was turned into faith, and she trusted Christ as her personal Lord and Savior. That is one reason we are commanded to preach the Bible, and remain confident in its power to change lives. Remember: *So then faith comes by hearing, and hearing by the Word of God* (Romans 10:17).

Next we discover that the Bible helps us effectively live for Christ. Paul made it clear that: *All Scripture is given by inspiration of God, and is profitable for doctrine, for reproof, for correction, for instruction in righteousness, that the man of God may be complete, thoroughly equipped for every good work* (II Timothy 3:16-17).

We can think of it like a football coach that is building a championship team. Doctrine is like the overall game plan. Reproof is telling us when we do something the wrong way. Correction is showing us the right way. Instruction in righteousness is working on something over and over until you can consistently do it right. It is the idea of something becoming "second nature" to you. In other words, you could practically "do it in your sleep" because you are so familiar with the fundamentals. This process equips you to effectively live for Christ.

Paul also issued a warning to essentially prepare for opposition. He said: *For the time will come when they will not endure sound doctrine, but according to their own desires because they have itching ears, they will heap up for themselves teachers; and they will turn their ears away from the truth, and be turned aside to fables* (II Timothy 4:3-4).

My friend, that time has come, and it is a tragic reality of our day. It reminds me of the Flip Wilson show that I used to watch as a kid. One particular skit was entitled, "Reverend Leroy and the Church of What's Happening Now!" We would sit in front of the television and laugh at the comedy. However, what was once a comedy has now become a sad tragedy in many churches. It seems that everything is in style with today's church except the preaching of the cross and the teaching of the Word of God. However, we must return to Biblical instruction and confront our culture, if we want to have any hope of saving the people of our culture.

I think of that moving scene in II Chronicles 34 when a discovery is made in the temple. It seems that the priests are doing a little spring-cleaning, and they come across an unfamiliar book. It is one they have vaguely heard about through the years, but have never taken the time to read it. In the process of time, the ancient book gets stored away with all the rest of the forgotten material.

However, as they open the book, they discover that it is the Law of God. Therefore, the priests brought the book to King Josiah to see what he wanted them to do with it. The king has the book read, and they discover how far removed the people have become from living as God intended. Consequently, a great revival broke out as the people returned to following the Word of God. In a similar way, it would be helpful if churches all over America were revived with biblical relevance.

I remember the time when Don came to see me at the church office. He wanted some advice for his business. However, Don was new to the church so I did a little "evangelistic probing" during our discussion. He had moved from Chicago and had attended a leading "seeker church" for five years. Unfortunately, far too much had been assumed about his salvation. During the visit, I explained the gospel and Don was gloriously saved. He will tell you today that the gospel was the most relevant need of his life at that time.

I believe that the bedrock of confidence is in knowing that God has spoken, and we must simply relay His message. However, the epitome of arrogance is the idea that we have something more creative to say than what God has commanded us to preach. I also believe, that anyone who has taken the time to genuinely study the Bible, will conclude that it is the most relevant book of all time.

I believe that the bedrock of confidence is in knowing that God has spoken...we must simply relay His message.

After all, it covers our greatest human need, which is forgiveness, and provides divine guidance for every area of our daily lives.

Imagine traveling toward the Tampa Bay Bridge on a dark night with your family. Suppose for a moment that the bridge is out and you were in grave danger. Let's also suppose that several groups are sponsoring "road side services" to help you travel comfortably. However, they do not want to offend you, so they do not tell you the bridge is out. After all, they want to be relevant and meet your "felt needs." They also want to guarantee that you and your family return to their "road side service."

You encounter all kinds of services as you travel. One group invites you to stop and study "time management" to help make your trip more efficient. Another group offers you "financial planning" so your trip will be more cost effective. Yet, another group wants you to stop so they can build up your "self esteem." Yes, these loving people want you to feel good on your trip.

Next, you discover that a group is offering a "family seminar" to help you get along together as you travel. Another group invites you to come "laugh with them." After all, if your current roadside service is boring, simply switch to their exciting and fun place! A final group even offers a "goal setting seminar." Yes this power-packed group wants you to fulfill your dreams as you travel!

Unfortunately, none of these groups tell you that the Tampa Bay Bride is out. May I suggest that the most relevant message for you and your family is that the bridge is out and you must take another road! In fact, the loving thing to do is to warn you of the disaster that is ahead if you do not get on another road!

In the same way, the most relevant message for the world is the bridge was knocked out between humanity and God. In fact, if we stay on the current road, we will face an eternal disaster. However, Jesus built a "new bridge" out of the "old rugged cross" that will connect us with God.

One summer during college, I worked for a roofing company. We were removing gravel off a flat roof of a major factory, and getting ready to put a new hot tar roof on it. In this process, we dangerously overloaded a weak section of the roof with too much gravel. Finally, a guy dumped another wheel barrel of gravel on the roof, and a twenty-foot section collapsed right in front of him.

All of the gravel fell down on to a transformer and knocked the electrical power out for most of the plant. He would have been killed had it not been for the fact that he was standing on a support beam. Everything in front of his eyes collapsed to the floor below his feet. His work for the day was destroyed, but his life was spared.

A similar scene is described in the third chapter of First Corinthians (verses 10-15). We find the sad reality of some people that will spend their time building on the wrong foundation. In the end, the leaders will be spared, but their "work of ministry" will burn before their eyes. It is a tragic tale of deception by being lured away from the message of the cross, and the preaching of the Word of God.

Our goal must be to avoid this mistake and faithfully proclaim the good news of the gospel. It is the most relevant message of every generation, and the great need of our culture today. May a new generation of preachers revive true relevance and become: *unashamed of the gospel of Christ, for it is the power of God to salvation for everyone who believes* (Romans 1:16).

CHAPTER 4

HIS LAST COMMAND;
OUR FIRST CONCERN

My Grandpa Schutz was a die-hard Cub fan. He "ate, drank, and slept" the Chicago Cubs. Initially, he put up a huge TV antenna in order to be able to pick up the WGN station, which broadcast the Cubs. Later on, when the satellite dishes became available, he installed one, and constantly cheered for his favorite baseball team. He was a loyal fan, and had a lifelong "love affair" with his beloved Cubbies.

Of course they broke his heart many times through the years. His greatest disappointment came during the "Great Depression" of 1969. That was the year the Chicago Cubs completely collapsed late in the season. They had a considerable lead going into the final month of the season. It looked like the Cubs were actually headed for the World Series. However, as only the Cubs can do, they lost several games down the stretch and blew the pennant race. The "Miracle Mets" won the National League Title, and went on to win World Series as well.

My Grandpa never forgave those "loveable losers" for that one! He would relive that disappointing season over and over through the years. In fact, if we wanted to "get a growl" out of Grandpa, we would simply bring up the famous season of 1969. It was a guaranteed way to "get him rolling" about the Cubs letting a golden opportunity slip away.

However, there was one time when the Cubs were not even remotely on his mind. It was the time my wife and I visited grandpa shortly before he went home to be with the Lord. It was not a time for idle conversation, and grandpa spoke about the thing that mattered the most to him. Tears began streaming down his face as he shared his concern for family members that needed Christ. I will never forget how he spoke with great passion from his deathbed. We joined hands with grandpa and grandma in a circle of believing prayer. We asked that God would hear the "cry of grandpa's heart" concerning his deep love for his family. It was an emotionally moving scene that is deeply embedded in my mind.

The last command of Christ was given in a similar context. Jesus was getting ready to return to the Father, and He shared His final instructions to the disciples. He spoke with great intensity and delivered a compelling message that called for total commitment to the mission. I am convinced that Christ had tremendous passion in His voice as He gave the final marching orders for the church. The "game-plan" for worldwide evangelization calls for total commitment to the cause of Christ. Therefore, His last command must be our first concern.

The context of the final challenge to the church is recorded in all four Gospels and the book of Acts. The message that flowed from the heart of Christ is clearly given in each account. His desire for the church to take the good news of the gospel to the entire world is clearly revealed. Jesus expects His Great Commission to be our mission.

Christ said: *Go therefore and make disciples of all the nations, baptizing them in the name of the Father and of the Son and of the Holy Spirit, teaching them to observe all things that I have commanded you; and lo, I am with you always, even to the end of the age* (Matthew 28:19-20).

He also stated the command in a similar way when He said: *Go into all the world and preach the gospel to every creature* (Mark 16:15). Then, in Luke 24: 47, Jesus said: *repentance and remission of sins should be preached in His name to all nations.* Jesus also alluded to the Great commission in John 20:21 when He said: *As the Father sent Me, I also send you.*

Finally, in Acts 1:8 we are told: *and you shall be witnesses to Me in Jerusalem, and in all Judea and Samaria, and to the end of the earth.* The emphasis of the Great Commission in all four Gospels, and the book of Acts is a clear indication of our purpose. Therefore, the Great Commission must be the mission for every ministry.

This leads us to the clarity of the command. Jesus said, "go into" the entire world; He did not tell us to "run from" the world. Therefore, I believe it is valuable to embrace the concept of infiltration instead of isolation as we reach out with the gospel. This emphasizes the importance of penetration into the community instead of separation from it. It is *Jesus said, "go into" the entire world; He did not tell us to "run from" the world.* the idea of "lighting a candle instead of cursing the darkness" as you build bridges of positive influence with the community.

Next we must understand the content of the command. The Great Commission is one command, which is to make disciples. This command is surrounded by three participles: going, baptizing and teaching. The "going" implies winning the lost to Christ. The "baptizing" implies the importance of public identification with Christ. The "teaching" is instructing the believer in the Word of God in order to follow Christ. Therefore, "making disciples" is the concept of reaching people for Christ, and helping Christians grow in their walk with the Lord.

A ministry that is guided by the Great Commission will have a genuine sense of biblical direction, which keeps the church from wandering aimlessly. It will also enable you to: focus your energy with unity, evaluate effectively, look to the future with a strategy, and embrace a sense of expectancy. This also increases the "confidence factor" with a contagious attitude that "the best is yet to come" in the exciting days ahead.

The Great Commission will also provide guidance in setting biblical goals for the ministry. Once the goals are developed from your objective of making disciples, the focus is shifted from simply being efficient, to the importance of being effective. After all, it does not make any sense to do something efficiently, if it should not be done at all.

In order to be the most effective in ministry, it is a good idea to have a target in mind as you carry out the Great Commission. Remember, if you aim at nothing, you will hit it every time. Therefore, I suggest focusing the ministry goals on reaching three types of people: the lost, the backslidden, and the positive church transfer.

Reaching out with the love of Christ will keep a church "fishing for the lost." This is much different than acting like "keepers of the aquarium." God has not com-

God has not commanded us to simply move believers from one "church tank" to another.

manded us to simply move believers from one "church tank" to another. Our primary objective is to help the lost come to faith in Christ. Therefore, it is important to keep "casting the gospel line" to those who need Christ.

The mission of Christ is clearly revealed in Luke 19:10 when Jesus said: *For the Son of Man has come to seek and to save that which was lost.* Therefore, "keeping the main thing, the main thing" needs to be the primary goal of every church. Reaching the lost is not only our biblical mandate; it also provides energy and enthusiasm for the church. It is always exciting for the congregation when the baptismal waters are flowing on a regular basis.

It is also valuable to restore the backslidden. These are people that once made a profession of faith, but have drifted away from the Lord. They simply need to be restored in their walk with the Lord. This could be considered "secondary evangelism" as you help them rekindle their walk with Christ. While they are not "resaved," they are "restored" to the faith with a fresh sense of spiritual vitality. Reaching the backslidden also provides a sense of excitement for the church. It always energizes a body of believers to see people reconnect with the Lord on a deeply personal level.

Finally, be willing to accept "positive church transfers" into your fellowship. Essentially, a positive church transfer is someone that embraces your purpose, and wants to "put their shoulder to the wheel" with you. They do not arrive with any "pre-set agenda" or "negative emotional baggage" as they unite with your fellowship. While the positive church transfer is not the primary target, it is beneficial to have "open arms" to them. After all, they can inject a fresh sense of positive energy, which will enhance the ministry.

Another principle that can be helpful is the concept of "household evangelism" as a strategy for outreach. This pattern runs all through the Bible. For example, Noah and his household were saved (Gen. 7:1). The nobleman and his household believed (John 4:53). Lydia and her household were saved (Acts 16:15). The "Philippian jailor" and his family came to Christ (Acts 16:33). The faith was handed down from grandmother to mother, to Timothy (II Timothy 1:5). The principle is clear, when you reach the head of the home, you can influence the entire family.

Remember, the family is the "heartbeat" of God. After all, God created the family unit before He created nations or even the church. Basically, healthy churches, stable communities, and strong nations are built with solid families. Therefore, aiming for the ultimate target of the head of the home can be an effective principle for evangelism. I suggest planning an occasional event to reach out to adults in order to help accomplish this goal.

Finally, one of the best aspects of Great Commission Guidance is the importance of balance in ministry. In the simplest sense, our task is to evangelize the unbeliever, and disciple the believer. Evangelism and discipleship are two sides of the same coin. It is not one at the expense of the other. We announce the good news of the gospel to the unbeliever, which helps them come to faith in Christ. We also instruct the believer in the Word of God, which helps them live by faith for Christ. The balance found in this approach will bless the church, and bring glory to God.

A couple weeks after having my final conversation with my grandpa, I spoke at his funeral. The memory of his heartfelt compassion for his family was embedded in my mind. The picture of the tears streaming down his face left an impression on me that will always remain. This man was so much more than a Cub fan; he was a champion of the faith. His only concern during the final days of his life was his earnest prayer that "every last loved one" would come to Christ.

As I shared the gospel at Grandpa's funeral, I relayed his desire for everybody to trust Christ as Savior. Following the service, we slowly drove to the cemetery in a lengthy funeral procession. Then came the time to "say goodbye" at the graveside. Our "pillar of faith" was laid to rest, and the "baton of faith" was passed on to us. It seemed like the world was moving in slow motion, as I stood in silence, and reflected on the tears of Grandpa.

Fortunately, through the years, his tears of compassion became joyful tears of conversion for several family members. The deathbed cry of a great Christian became a battle cry for the Great Commission. Yes, sowing in tears leads to reaping with joy, as we follow Christ and keep: His last command, our first concern.

CHAPTER 5

COURAGE TO IMPLEMENT CHANGE

L eadership is not for cowards. Period. Being a "change agent" is not for the "faint-hearted" because implementing change is a delicate and dangerous business. It is impossible to please everybody, and some will naturally resist change. However, if I can borrow a famous line from a Godfather movie: "This is the business we've chosen!"

Therefore, the courageous leader will want to claim the promise of God as found in Joshua 1:9. God said: *Be strong and of good courage; do not be afraid, nor be dismayed, for the Lord your God is with you wherever you go.* This valuable promise is not just for Joshua of old; it will also empower us today.

> **Leadership is not for cowards. Period.**

Unfortunately, too many churches would rather die a comfortable death, instead of courageously making changes to live a vibrant life. Too often churches are willing to "maintain the status quo" and fail, instead of implementing changes to succeed. The idea of using the purpose of the Great Commission as a guide for evaluating our effectiveness is seldom considered.

For example, let's say that you have a ministry in the church that has long lost its effectiveness. However, somebody's "Aunt Matilda" originally started that program. Therefore, even though "Aunt Matilda" has been in the grave for over twenty years, somehow we would "offend her" if we abandoned that ministry. Consequently, the church remains "loyal to Aunt Matilda" and hobbles along with a failing program.

The sad reality is that they have lost sight of why Aunt Matilda originally started the program. She probably recognized a need during her time, and designed or discovered a program to meet the need. However, it was not a particular program that originally "got the ball rolling." It was the purpose of meeting a specific need. In fact, if "Aunt Matilda" were alive today, she would probably recognize a different need and "lead the charge" to implement a new program. That is what leaders do, and Aunt Matilda was undoubtedly a leader.

Another problem is dealing with "Uncle Bob" who has held a particular leadership position for years. There is only one problem; "Uncle Bob" is unqualified to effectively handle the assignment. He is a nice guy that means well, and nobody wants to hurt his feelings. Consequently, we allow "Uncle Bob" to hinder the growth and the effectiveness of the ministry.

Then there is that couple that we all know as: "Mr. and Mrs. Do Everything" in ministry. Nobody else gets to do much of anything because "Mr. and Mrs. Do Everything" think they can do everything! Somehow through the years, "Mr. and Mrs. Do Everything" carried the torch when nobody else wanted to carry it. However in the process of rescuing the church, they became the bottleneck of the church. Consequently, many qualified people "sit on the sidelines" and watch "Mr. and Mrs. Do Everything" refuse to give up much of anything. They have taken an unhealthy "possessive ownership" of the church that becomes an unhealthy situation for the church.

Unfortunately, in an indirect way, the mission of the church has digressed into: keeping "Aunt Matilda" from rolling over in her grave, protecting the feelings of "Uncle Bob" as he struggles with a leadership position, and feeding the pride of "Mr. and Mrs. Do Everything" as they live in their imaginary bubble that they are the only ones capable of doing most things. My friend, the "stakes are too high" to allow this kind of futility to continue. It is simply unacceptable for dying churches to remain comfortable about the fact that people are dying without Christ. Therefore, the time has come to inspire the courage to implement changes to be more effective in reaching people for Christ.

In order to accurately evaluate the success or a failure of an area of ministry, it is crucial to focus on effectiveness not just efficiency. Being efficient is the idea of "doing things right." However, being effective is focusing on "doing the right things." After all, it is useless to do something efficiently when it should not be done at all! This brings us right back to using the Great Commission as your guide for the evaluation process. When it comes to the importance of succeeding in a Great Commission Ministry, I am reminded of a famous line from the movie Apollo 13: "Failure is not an option!"

This leads to the importance of "timing" in the process of implementing change. Timing is everything. This is only good common sense. Consequently, there are a few basic principles to keep in mind as you *Timing is everything.* attempt to implement change.

For example, the right idea with the wrong timing will lead to frustration. Too often a good idea gets "shot down" because the leader did not have enough common sense to bring it up at the right time. It can be the best idea in the world, but if your timing is off, the idea will die on the vine. Simply choose to "live and learn" from the frustrating experience, and "do your home work" a little better next time.

On the other hand, the wrong idea with the right timing will lead to humiliation. Perhaps the people are ripe and ready for change. They realize that an aspect of the ministry is not working and something has to be done. The only problem is that you offer a bad idea. They run with it and it fails miserably. The best thing to do is to "eat a little humble pie" and learn from the experience. The failure does not have to be fatal if you determine to not "trip over the same rock twice" and grow in wisdom as a leader.

Another scenario is the wrong idea with the wrong timing. This will lead to devastation. This is a scenario where the people are very resistant to change, and a bad idea gets pushed through anyway. The leader winds up standing there with "egg all over their face" as the whole thing blows up. This is a learning curve you want to avoid at all cost. This kind of mistake can cause your leadership credibility to "take a hit" with the people. It takes time to recover from this type of ministry blunder so don't get "trigger happy" about making other changes in the near future. Your patience on future changes will also help you reestablish some all important leadership credibility.

The ideal situation is having the right idea with the right timing. This will lead to successful innovation. The time for change has come and the people are eager for something new. A good idea is presented and well received. The people embrace the idea and take some positive ownership of the vision. The change is made and the ministry flourishes as a result of the change.

This results in a blessing for everybody involved. The ministry moves forward in a positive direction and the church is more effective in accomplishing its mission. It is very satisfying as a leader to implement the right idea at the right time, and for the right reason. The church is better off with the successful innovation and your leadership influence is affirmed as well. Therefore, always remember that "timing is everything" for successful innovation.

I would offer a final suggestion on the subject of making changes. An old, but wise saying goes as follows: "Never tear down a fence until you have taken the time to find out the reason it was put up in the first place." That ancient principle of wisdom can provide some valuable insight for our modern world.

We have made many strategic changes at New Life that have proven successful, and I want to take this opportunity to share one. The original name, First Southern Baptist Church, was based on a different strategy for growth. Prior to 1985, the primary target was reaching Southern Baptist people as they moved to our community. So the church put the denominational name "front and center" with the hope of attracting believers of "like faith and order."

However, when the church called me as pastor, we shifted our strategy for outreach. We immediately began to emphasize the importance of reaching the lost for Christ in our community. We developed the concept of infiltration instead of isolation, in order to influence our community with the gospel. Therefore, since the term "Southern Baptist" was not helping us accomplish our mission, we changed our name.

This decision was also made after I had served as pastor for seven years. This is significant because it allowed me ample time to develop a "proven track record" of trusted leadership with the congregation. It also gave us time to demonstrate our commitment to the community. We were also relocating our church campus, so it was a natural opportunity to begin establishing a new identity in a new community.

Most importantly, our motive was based on our mission of the Great Commission. Our goal was to remove a roadblock for the sake of the gospel. We wanted to represent our message of the New Life that God offers through faith in Jesus Christ. It also paved the way to further influence our community with our emphasis on positive faith.

A final aspect for the name change was the fact that we were building a new church at a new location. This automatically changed our church address from Mishawaka to Osceola, and the "table was set" for changing our name. Therefore, the timing was perfect and the change was made. It was the right idea with the right timing, and it resulted in a successful innovation.

I do want to point out that a "successful innovation" does not mean that everybody is always happy. After all, every time the "train leaves the station" not everybody gets on board. In fact, if you waited for everyone to be on board, the "gospel train" would never roll down the tracks. Consequently, you cannot worry about being a "people pleaser" because "souls hang in the balance." Therefore, the "Great Commission Leader" must not allow a few negative people to stop the positive progress of a Great Commission Ministry. Remember, leadership is not for cowards. Period.

Every time the "train leaves the station" not everybody gets on board.

CHAPTER 6

IDEAS OVER INSTITUTIONS

Yesterday people were loyal to institutions. Today they are loyal to ideas. Yesterday people joined the military to fight a war simply because the institution of government (Uncle Sam) asked for a commitment. Today they are more likely to fight for a cause if they believe the idea is worth defending. Yesterday people remained married because of a strong belief in the institution of marriage. Today they are more interested in the idea of a meaningful relationship, and may keep searching until they find one.

Yesterday people were more likely to support only one political institution (Republican or Democrat). Today they are more *Yesterday people were* inclined to embrace a candidate because *loyal to institutions.* they like his or her ideas, regardless of the political party represented. *Today they are* Yesterday people were loyal to a reli-*loyal to ideas.* gious institution of a clearly defined denomination. Today they are more loyal to the idea of a clearly defined spiritual mission, and less drawn to a denomination.

For the local church, this can be viewed as either an obstacle to overcome, or an opportunity to capitalize on. It will all depend upon whether you are trying to build a ministry on the loyalty to an institution, or the loyalty of an idea. If you choose institutional loyalty as your strategy for ministry, your opportunity for outreach will be greatly limited. You may provide a comfortable "haven of rest" for the "loyal remnant" of your denomination, but you will miss out on a great open door for the gospel. Especially in areas of the country where your denomination may be less known. One major adversity, may be the glaring reality, that there may not even be enough people of your "denominational flavor" to sustain an effective ministry. This "institutional loyalty approach" will also contribute to an existing adversity, which is a cultural wall that has already formed between your church and the community.

However, if you choose the "loyalty to an idea approach" to ministry, your potential will greatly increase for effective outreach. This is because people are more open today than ever before to try a church that will meet their spiritual needs. The lack of denominational loyalty can be

Our open-minded religious culture has created an incredible opening for the gospel.

used to your advantage if you capitalize on the opportunity. Our open-minded religious culture has created an incredible opening for the gospel. God has given an unprecedented open door for us to share the good news with people that need the Lord. The wise church will seize this moment in history, and capitalize on the tremendous opportunity to tell "His Story" of love and forgiveness.

With this in mind, I highly recommend, "losing denominational labels" for the sake of reaching the lost. After all, the only label found in the New Testament is the word "Christian" to describe followers of Christ. The Bible says: *And the disciples were first called Christians in Antioch* (Acts 11:26). Most other labels that have developed through the years turn into walls that keep people out, instead of bridges to invite people into the church.

Therefore, I suggest removing all denominational labels from your church name, literature, signs, and web site. Believers will discover your church if it is worth finding, and unbelievers are not interested in denominational labels. Once again, it is important to keep in mind that, in today's culture people are loyal to ideas, instead of institutions. Consequently, if people believe in your mission, they will be attracted to your ministry.

If you desire to let the people of your denomination know that a church for them is available in the community, you can always use a familiar denominational symbol. For example, Southern Baptists have a very recognizable symbol of the world, cross, and the Bible to represent their denomination. Most other denominations have some type of symbol that represents them as well. Therefore, placing the appropriate symbol in a visible place, allows people that are specifically looking for a particular denomination, know that their "flavor of faith" is available.

By the way, the largest Protestant Denomination in the United States, the Southern Baptist Convention, has wisely shifted their emphasis in literature sales. The implementation of the name "LifeWay Christian Resources" is more appealing to a broader Christian market, which has strategically opened the door for greater evangelical influence. For example, the LifeWay Christian Bookstore in downtown Chicago, undoubtedly has more "evangelical traffic" because the word "Christian" is now the emphasis, instead of a "Baptist" bookstore. In a similar way, a local church can have greater evangelical influence when denominational labels are not the major point of emphasis.

One final suggestion on the subject of "losing the denominational label." It can be wise to reduce the rhetoric from the pulpit on what your denomination is doing. Once again, the visitor seldom cares, and there are other ways to keep the regular attendee informed. It is easy to point out that our missionaries are responding to a tragedy during a natural disaster, etc. The member knows what you are saying and the visitor feels good that your church cares about the needs of others. You can get the message across without continually "waving a denominational label" from the pulpit.

Let me say at this point that I am not even hinting at the notion of pulling out of a denomination. It is obviously beneficial to work together with other churches of like faith for the purpose of worldwide evangelization. However, on a local level, I do not believe it is necessary, and certainly not helpful, to wave a "denominational banner" all around. In fact, in some cases it can even be detrimental to our cause for Christ. To me, it simply boils down to the Biblical principle of *becoming all things to all men that we might by all means win some* (I Corinthians 9:22).

I remember an occasion when I was watching a high school baseball game, and the former varsity football coach sat down beside me. He is of the Catholic Faith, and he asked me how things were going at the Baptist Church. I responded that we have removed the word Baptist from our name. He was curious for the reason, so I simply told him that the word "Christian" is the only label found in the New Testament. Therefore, we have removed all labels and simply refer to ourselves as: New Life, Home of Positive Faith.

He responded very favorably to the idea. He and his wife have also been our guests at the church on Friend Day. They loved the service and stated they were "moved by the message" and enjoyed the upbeat music as well. This was an amazing statement from his wife because New Life is the only non-Catholic church she has ever attended. I could list many other examples of people, with a similar background, that we have eventually led to Christ. Therefore, I am in favor of the idea of "losing a label" for the sake of the lost.

Another valuable concept of "ideas over institutions" is the importance of structuring the ministry based on the biblical functions, instead of a traditional format. For example, the five biblical functions of a local church are revealed in Acts 2:41-42, and are as follows: Evangelism, Bible Teaching, Christian Fellowship, Worship, and the Ministry of Prayer. It is valuable to realize that the biblical functions of the church are timeless, but the traditional format may need to adjust with the times.

Let me share a classic example of an innovative idea to accomplish a biblical function turned into a traditional format that is still clung to by some today. The Sunday Evening Service was created in the 19th century when Charles Haddon Spurgeon came up with an innovative idea for evangelism. The churches in London England had begun shifting toward liberal theology. The movement became known as the "Great Downgrade" and had devastating results on many churches. The need for personal salvation was under attack because liberal theologians were teaching universal redemption. This is the dangerous heresy that all people will be saved regardless of what they personally believe.

Therefore, Spurgeon began the Sunday evening service to preach the gospel. This service did not conflict with regular church attendance in other places because nobody held Sunday evening services before that time. Therefore, people were free to attend their own local churches on Sunday morning, and could attend the London Tabernacle on Sunday evening. This was a completely knew idea for evangelism.

In fact, the attendance grew so large on Sunday evening that Spurgeon had to move the service to the Surrey Theatre. It was the only building in London that could handle the enormous crowds. For example, the attendance at Spurgeon's church was around 2000 on an average Sunday morning. However, on an average Sunday evening the crowds were over 10,000 in attendance. Therefore, the innovative decision to move a sacred service to a secular building was made. This was a radical idea for that time in church history.

However, through the years the Sunday evening service was simply adopted into the traditional format for many churches. In fact, to eliminate the Sunday evening service is a sign of "liberalism" to some churches today. The original idea of the biblical function of evangelism is seldom considered as a "Sunday evening target" anymore, but the traditional format has been "chiseled in stone" for many churches. Unfortunately, some refuse to examine a fresh idea to be more effective in ministry. As a result, a church becomes bound to a traditional format, and blocked from accomplishing a biblical function.

The mid-week "prayer meeting" can be traced to a similar tradition. For years, churches did not necessarily come together during the week. However, during the first and second "Great Awakenings" of our spiritual heritage, the "Prayer Service" was born. Christians gathered at the church during the week and fervently prayed for revival in the church, and the salvation of the lost. As a result, God moved in a powerful way. However, today we simply believe it important to have some type of activity going on during the week. Once again, the traditional format of mid-week activities has become the gauge of spiritual life. Therefore, we may need to reconsider some innovative ways to accomplish the ministry function of prayer.

Bottom line, we should always evaluate the ministry in terms of carrying out the five biblical functions, instead of clinging to a traditional format. It is imperative that we think in terms of the "idea" of making disciples, instead of simply embracing the "institution" of church life. Otherwise, we can become like a furnace that has the fan blowing, but the fire has gone out. Remember, people will warm up to an idea, and walk away from a cold institution. The reason is simply this: yesterday, people were loyal to instutions, but today they are loyal to ideas.

CHAPTER 7

BUILDING BRIDGES

One afternoon, the principal of a local elementary school, called and asked if I would coach their flag football team. I politely responded that I would get back with him in a few minutes. I called my wife and asked what she thought of the idea. Cindi said: "Mike it sounds like a good opportunity to build a bridge to the community." It also gave me an additional blessing of coaching my son Joseph, who was in the fifth grade at the time. I called the principal, and agreed to help the school by serving as their coach.

Building bridges is a labor of love. The goal is to help the church connect with the community in a positive way. The strategy is based on the principle of *becoming all things to all people, that we might by all means save some* (I Corinthians 9:22). It is the idea of the church taking an interest in the community, not simply trying to get the community interested in the church. The result of building bridges is a positive influence in the community, and a positive impact on the church.

The goal is to help the church connect with the community in a positive way.

I was exited for the God-given opportunity to build a bridge through coaching, and recruited a couple of other guys to help. We set a few "bridge building goals" to effectively accomplish our purpose. First, we wanted to keep it a positive experience for the boys by allowing them to have fun! We also wanted to help them develop a healthy sense of confidence, as they learned to believe in themselves. Next, we wanted to relate football to the "game of life" and teach the boys principles of "championship character."

Naturally, we also wanted to provide some basic instruction in the game of football.

When 55 boys showed up for the first practice, we immediately discovered the importance of developing a game plan to provide playing time for everyone. I definitely did not want to have a: first string, second string, etc. After all, no elementary child should ever be made to feel like a "second stringer" on or off the field.

Therefore, we made a decision to use the names of college teams for the offense, and pro teams for the defense. It was exciting to shout: Irish or Wolverine offense, or Bears, Cowboys, or Packers defense, and watch eleven excited boys charge the field to play. This excitement was repeated all through out the game as various units were called into action. Everybody was included and felt a tremendous sense of belonging to the team.

We even received local TV coverage as the boys went undefeated and won the City Championship! The season was capped off with an Award Ceremony, and hundreds of parents and grandparents attended. We took the time to publicly compliment every member of the team, as each boy received his individual trophy with pride. We also presented a plaque to the principal, which included the words: With God all things are possible.

We coached four years in a row, and accomplished the same results each season. Most importantly, we had the privilege of leading several families to Christ. In fact, many of them still attend New Life. Eventually, we helped launch the elementary tackle football program, and moved on to other bridge building opportunities.

When the head football coach of Mishawaka High School asked me to deliver a pre-game motivational speech, another community connection was made. This evolved into the role of Team Chaplain. I have the privilege of providing "game day inspiration" for the varsity football team during the season. It has proven to be a tremendous bridge for the gospel.

This same bridge building principle has expanded into another area high school. My son Michael, who serves as our Executive

Pastor, has been given the opportunity to provide "character chalk talks" to the Penn High School wrestling team. It is amazing how God continues to use this positive approach to open doors, and influence our community with positive faith.

In order to build bridges of love, we must focus on making a positive contact with the community. It is important to help the congregation think in terms of a Great Commission Ministry. Do not assume that it comes naturally for the church. Provide some practical instruction in the concept of "bridge building" for outreach.

For example, if you have a volunteer coach or two in the church, help them see the opportunity to build a bridge for the gospel. Provide a few practical pointers on how to be an encourager by keeping everything positive and uplifting. Help them understand the needs of children to develop a positive self-esteem. Teach the coach to gather the team together after every game, and compliment each player for some positive contribution. This will draw the players and parents to the coach like a magnet.

Perhaps even give a few tips on the opportunity to include a brief (five minute maximum) "character chalk talk" in a weekly practice. Parents will love it as they see their children learn values like honesty, loyalty, integrity, hard work, hustle, teamwork, and respect. It is a great way to develop "champions in the game of life" and build a bridge for the gospel.

Include some instruction on how to recognize "hungry hearts" in this process. It can be as simple as paying attention to those that gravitate your way during the season. Look for people that do not attend church anywhere, and at an appropriate time (don't rush it), invite to: Friend Day, Bible School, Church Camp, Youth Activities, golf outings, etc. We have seen many come to Christ with this exact "bridge building model."

This strategy can be repeated in many different arenas of community contact such as: Boy Scouts, Girl Scouts, ballet, bowling and golf leagues, gymnastics, hunting, fishing, etc. Basically, whatever the people are involved in, encourage them to be a positive person, and build a bridge for the gospel. Then at the right opportunity, seize the moment and invite someone to church. God will use it to reach people for Christ.

Other ways to build bridges are through community involvement. Enlist members to donate a little "elbow grease" to clean up a local park or community building. Some may enjoy volunteering at a local hospital, nursing home, or a homeless shelter. Others may "lend a helping hand" to organizations like Habitat for Humanity.

Anything that involves the people in community service is healthy for the congregation. It promotes a spirit of goodwill in the community, and builds a positive bridge for gospel opportunities. I guarantee that a little brainstorming on this subject, and your church will think of many ways to build bridges of love to connect with your community.

We have also developed a few community-wide events that have been wonderful bridges. For example, we designed a Little League Sunday at the church. We invited all the teams from the local ballparks to attend New Life for a special service. We included a gift for every ball player in attendance. We also donated new equipment to every park that had the President of the League represented. We included some special drawings, and honored a few people with appreciation plaques as well. Following the service, we provided a free hotdog and crackerjack lunch, and an instructional clinic.

Our theme was: Learn character today and lead the community tomorrow. Our Championship Character Award was given to a twelve-year-old boy for cheering on his team, even though he was unable to play due to a broken arm. We also gave an appreciation plaque to the District Administrator for her many years of volunteer service. In time, the District Administer, and several others trusted Christ.

Another event we have successfully developed is an outdoor Patriotic Celebration, which we now call our Freedom Festival. This idea was born after the terrorist attack on September 11, 2001. The following summer we hosted a major event that resembled an old fashioned Fourth of July celebration. We included free carnival rides to attract families, and then honored: government officials, local law enforcement, military personnel, fire fighters, emergency medical technicians, etc. The celebration included a Patriotic Concert, and a patriotic speech, with a gospel presentation. We capped off the evening with an exciting fireworks display!

The first year we had over 2500 in attendance. By the third year, the crowd swelled to 5000! Then, we added a "new wrinkle" when the lead guitar player from the Buckinghams, affirmed his faith in Christ at New Life. We recruited Dave to play golden oldies music of the sixties and seventies. His final song, right before my message was "He Ain't Heavy; He's My Brother" by the Hollies. Countless baby boomers were "dialed in" for the gospel presentation. It was an incredible bridge building event!

It is also important to remain open to the contacts your people have with the community. For example, one of our members, Jill, served as the choreographer for a local high school performing Godspell. The musical is loosely based on a modern rendition of the Gospel of Matthew.

Therefore, we invited them to perform a couple of scenes at our church one Sunday evening. At the conclusion, I spoke for fifteen minutes on the theme of Matthew. It was a great opportunity to go from the "cradle to the cross" and explain the gospel. Then we gave each student a complimentary copy of the New Testament. It was powerful.

We also use the "feed them and they will come" bridge building principle. We provide complimentary pasta dinners for various local high school teams. My wife is Italian, and her secret recipe for spaghetti sauce is incredible! Her Grandpa came here from Sicily when he was twelve, and her Grandma was "born in the harbor" of Ellis Island. Believe me, the mouth-watering recipe from the "old country" is a big hit! It has helped create many positive inroads with the families of our area athletes.

Another thing to consider is the "hot button" of your community. For example, basketball is big in Indiana, so we hosted a three-on-three tournament. We set up portable hoops all around the parking lot, and invited various age groups to participate. We included a trophy presentation and a brief gospel message.

It is also wise to consider national trends. For example, soccer is the fastest growing sport in the country. Therefore, we looked for a way to capitalize on this national trend for community outreach. Initially, Upward Soccer was our answer. Eventually, we developed our own program called Positive Faith Soccer, with hundreds of children participating.

In order to promote "positive faith" in our community, we created a 15-minute radio broadcast called Power for Living. It is aired on secular stations and geared for the community. We chose not to broadcast on Christian stations because Jesus said: *Those who are well have no need of a physician* (Matthew 9:12). Incidentally, the broadcast has been a positive bridge building tool with many of our Catholic friends.

It is also important to build a few "draw bridges" as well. Sometimes you may do something for a few years, and then draw it back. Give it a rest for a period of time, and then bring it back with a new look. This keeps it from becoming "old hat" to the community. The main thing is to remain focused on the mission, but flexible with your methods.

The ministry is about people. Building bridges of love is designed to help the congregation connect with the community. After all, if we want to reach our community for Christ, we must remain in contact with people who need the Lord. The church must focus on infiltration instead of isolation. This principle is so engrained in our people that it has become a part of our DNA as a congregation. Countless people have trusted Christ through our bridge building efforts, and several united with New Life.

The church must focus on infiltration instead of isolation.

How valuable is it to build bridges to the community? In 2006, a lawyer on the Mishawaka school board decided the team chapels violated the separation of church and state. He issued a statement and cancelled the program. I asked the coach if he wanted the team chapels to continue. He was definitely in favor of keeping the positive influence of championship character principles in his football program.

I scheduled a collective meeting with the school lawyer, principal, and athletic director. Our staff went to prayer, and I "went to bat" for the team. At the beginning of the meeting, I placed four trophies on the table. They were the same kind of trophies that each boy received from the championship flag football teams years ago. I shared the character principles that we taught, and mentioned the names of several of those guys, who had gone into the military to defend our freedom.

Our conversation included a brief presentation of the positive influence our church members have in the community. I proceeded with the drug problem that our public high schools are facing and made this statement to the group: "If I was sitting where you men are sitting, I would look for help in developing character wherever I could find it." I asked on behalf of our community, to not deny these young men this character building opportunity. In an amazing answer to prayer, and a tribute to the principle of bridge building, the lawyer reversed his decision.

Today, the school has a new coach and new athletic director, but the same tradition continues. At the request of the team, we provide Game Day Inspiration. Make no mistake about it, building positive bridges of love, gives the church an opportunity to influence the community with positive faith.

CHAPTER 8

CLOSED MINDS MUST NOT BE ALLOWED TO SHUT OPEN DOORS

Compassionate people build bridges for the gospel. Critical people blow up bridges for the gospel. Closed-minded people cannot even recognize an opportunity to build a bridge for the gospel. Further more, closed-minded people do not even care about the bridges others are building for the gospel. Worst of all, some closed-minded people will actually attempt to shut the very doors that compassionate "bridge builders" are opening for the gospel. This is tragic because eternal destinies hang in the balance. Therefore, closed minds must not be allowed to shut open doors!

For example, when we began the "flag football ministry" with a local elementary, we needed transportation for the away games. Since the away games were very short trips to elementary schools in town, we thought it would be great to use the church bus. Our Associate Pastor drove the bus, and 55 excited boys (and adult coaches) would "whoop and holler" across town! The parents loved it, and we believed it was positive advertisement for the church as well.

Compassionate people build bridges for the gospel. Critical people blow up bridges for the gospel.

However, one "closed-minded brother" saw it differently. He thought the pastor had "no business spending his time" coaching flag football. After all, he was "paid by the church" to serve the congregation. Then, to top it off, using the church bus for something "unrelated to the ministry" was cause for more concern.

I was unaware of the criticism, but eventually it was brought to my attention in a positive way. One Sunday, Jerry, a faithful member, and the town barber, came up to me and said: "Pastor, I want you to know that I think it is great that you are coaching the elementary flag football team." He also gave me a generous amount of money, and instructed me to fill up the church bus on him. He went on to say that he would provide the gas money any time we used the bus to transport the team. I asked him why he was doing it, and he responded that he wanted to "close the mouth" of a negative critic.

A couple years later, I was asked to preach the funeral of the grandmother of one of the boys from the team. She actually served in the capacity of his mother because the grandparents were raising Matt. They attended our church one Easter Sunday and heard the gospel message. A few months later, one of our members led her to Christ on her deathbed. I was then called upon to preach the funeral.

A couple of weeks after the funeral, Matt, his sister Maria, and Grandpa Harlow made professions of faith, and were baptized at New Life. A few years later, I also had the honor of performing the wedding for Harlow, when God graciously brought Sarah into his life. Eventually, Matt attended Moody Bible Institute, and went into full-time ministry.

In time, many people came to Christ as a direct result of building a bridge through flag football. Several of those families still attend our church on a regular basis. Many others associated with the team will attend on special occasions. Needless to say, it was a good investment of time and gas money. Yes, closed minds must not be allowed to shut open doors.

We also had a small "critical corner" of closed-minded people that did not understand our Little League Sunday. However, we built a positive bridge to the community anyway. In fact, I would like to share "the rest of the story" concerning the District Administrator that trusted Christ as her Savior.

A few years after attending on Little League Sunday, her husband was dying of cancer. The family asked me to visit him in the hospital, and he personally asked me to preach his funeral. During the hospital visit, he shared of his experience of trusting Christ as a teenager at church camp. It was a touching moment in ministry.

Later, his funeral was held at New Life. The man had coached varsity softball for girls at Mishawaka for many years, and had influenced many lives in the process. The church was packed with school officials, and former players that loved him dearly. The funeral service that day not only brought comfort to the family, but it also confirmed another influential bridge that New Life had built to the community. It was a good thing that a few closed-minds were not allowed to shut the door on Little League Sunday.

There were also a select few that wondered about the value of a brief 15-minute radio program on secular stations. However, it has opened tremendous doors for the gospel as well. One miraculous story is of a woman in the hospital dying of cancer. She kept asking for "Mike" as her children reviewed their "family tree" to discover whom she wanted. Finally, she mentioned that she listened to Mike on the radio.

Someone in the room happened to be familiar with our broadcast, and asked if she wanted me to come to the hospital? A weak smile came across her face as she nodded in agreement. They called the church, and I had the privilege of helping her trust Christ. One week later, my daughter sang, and I shared the gospel, at the "standing room only" funeral service of my radio listener friend.

Jesus had His critics known as the Pharisees, and they are still hanging around the church today. Jesus stated that *they do not have the love of God in them* (John5: 42), and the **Sadly, their closed minds can shut doors that lead to heaven.** same holds true today. They are blinded to open doors for the gospel because their emphasis is not on people that need Christ. Too often, they only look at the cost of a bridge building event, and lose sight of the countless people that will hear the gospel.

Sadly, their closed minds can shut doors that lead to heaven. Consequently, there is far too much at stake to allow these types of people to influence the ministry. After all, eternity hangs in the balance for lost people all around us.

I cannot help but share one more example of the importance of this subject. His name was Cole. He first came in contact with the New Life ministry in the Spring of 2002, when he participated in our three-on-three basketball tourney. A few weeks later he attended our fireworks display. That evening my son Michael handed Cole a flier, and invited him to youth camp. The teenagers were leaving for camp in the morning, so he had very little time to decide.

The next morning, to our delight, Cole showed up ready to go. He was heading off "sight unseen" to the Real Power Youth Camp designed by New Life. That week, he had the time of his life, and most importantly, he made a life-changing decision. Cole responded to the gospel and trusted Christ as his Lord and Savior. After camp, His parents reaffirmed their faith, and later on, his sister made a private profession of faith.

However, during Thanksgiving weekend of 2002, Cole became mysteriously ill. The doctors were initially puzzled by his sickness. Soon, he was in the hospital fighting for his life, as many went to God in prayer. However, on December 4, 2002, Cole went home to be with the Lord. He died of a sudden illness at the young age of sixteen.

The principal of his public school personally requested our pastoral staff to minister to the students. In response to his gracious invitation, we provided prayer and counseling for the hurting students. It was a very sad scene to see the many broken hearted young people that were overwhelmed with grief.

On Friday evening, December 6, 2002, the viewing for Cole was held at New Life. Several hundred people responded in love to the hurting family. That evening, a very moving slide presentation was shown in memory of Cole. It told the beautiful story of a very loving family relationship. That memory is deeply embedded in my mind.

On Saturday, December 7, 2002, the church was packed as family and friends gathered to honor the life of Cole. His family was hurting deeply, and the church and community offered loving support. We claimed the precious promise and foundational truth that Cole is in heaven. The Bible is clear concerning the death of a Christian that: *To be absent from the body is to be present with the Lord* (II Corinthians 5:8). It was a very sad time of incredible sorrow, but we took comfort in the fact that we will see him again.

Later in the day, my wife and I sat in our car in the church parking lot. After several minutes of quiet reflection, I turned to Cindi and told her thank you. She asked why I was thanking her? I told her that I am very thankful for her faithful and loving encouragement. All through the years, she has helped me "stay the course" in our bridge building ministry.

The brief life of Cole is a life-long reminder to me of the value of building bridges for the gospel. As pastor, it also reminds me of the importance of not allowing a few closed minds to shut the many open doors for the gospel. I thank God for our loving congregation that embraces the vision of building bridges of love. I believe many in heaven will also say "thank you" for keeping an open mind, and walking through open doors to share God's love.

CHAPTER 9

FACE THE MUSIC

In May of 2004 the Cramer family proudly sat in the historic Moody Church. It was a great moment as we anxiously waited for our oldest son Michael, to receive his diploma. He was graduating from the Moody Bible Institute with a degree in pastoral ministry. As people gathered in the auditorium before the ceremony began, the organist was providing some background music. The multi-million dollar pipe organ was being played so loud that our seats literally vibrated. The organist was playing the great hymns of the faith with tremendous zeal.

At one point, our son Jacob, who was in high school at the time, leaned over and said to me: "Man Dad, this music sounds creepy." I smiled and asked him not to say that too loudly around Moody. After all, some of those "super saints" would have been outraged to hear such blasphemous words about the pipe organ sounding creepy!

However, to some the sound of the pipe organ reminds them of the "creepy music" that might be played as background music during an intense scene of a horror movie. To others, the pipe organ may remind them of the light-hearted TV show, the Adams Family. To others, it resonates a deeply spiritual feeling about the great hymns of the faith.

I must admit that as I observed the crowd, I could not help but wonder how some of those same believers would feel if a praise band was playing music at the same volume. Perhaps they would feel like that "noise" was far too loud? Some would even consider it a travesty to have music so loud in a church. I am confident that if the same music was played at the same volume, but with different instrumentation, some would think it was not reverent. They might think it was disrespectful to the "sacred sanctuary" of the church. All I am saying is that music is very generational and deeply personal. Too often, it gets labeled "spiritual" or "unspiritual" based on style instead of substance.

On another occasion, we had gathered at a Sunday morning worship service at the Word of Life Bible Institute, where our daughter Hannah was attending. During the offertory special the pianist played a lively hymn with great gusto. Her hands moved up and down the keys as she played the piano with a tremendous dramatic flare. It was a beautiful instrumental song that touched the crowd in a deeply meaningful way.

Too often, it gets labeled "spiritual" or "unspiritual" based on style instead of substance.

Once again, I found myself smiling inside. I could not help but wonder how the same crowd would have responded to a praise band playing with such enthusiasm. Just suppose that: the drummer was twirling the sticks; the base player jumping up and down with joy; the keyboardist leaning in and pounding hard on the keys, and the lead guitar player down on one knee putting everything into the song! There is no doubt in my mind that some of the same people that enjoyed the dramatic flare being played on the piano, would accuse a praise band of "showing off" with such antics.

My observation is simply that most people have a favorable or unfavorable response to music based upon their own personal taste. Some like it traditional and others prefer contemporary, but both should consider the substance of the lyrics, not just the style of the instrumentation. After all, the style of instrumentation will usually vary based on generational taste, cultural background, and geographical location.

One of the things that will identify your church is the music that is emphasized in the church. If you want to appeal to a generation that has been heavily influenced by rock and roll, I suggest incorporating contemporary Christian music into your services. The instrumentation of a quality praise band (drums, guitars, keyboard, etc.) will help you connect with your community. Keep the music upbeat and exciting. Music designed for a funeral belongs at the funeral, not in a Dynamic Positive Faith Worship Service.

I must admit, we "drug our feet" for quite some time on this one. I had wanted to move forward with more contemporary music for several years, but we did not have the personnel for a praise band. I have always believed that the only thing worse than no praise band is a bad praise band. Therefore, it was important that we picked the right time to effectively implement the change. Don't get me wrong, we had quality soloists, and a very good gospel quartet, but our music had become too limited in its generational appeal.

However, this all began to change one evening over a slice of pizza. My wife and I were hosting our good friends, Ron and Leslie, when the subject turned to contemporary Christian music. Eventually, Leslie turned to Ron and asked if he was ever going to tell the pastor about his life before becoming a Christian. I quietly braced myself for some "confession of the soul" from one of our deacons. Fortunately, Ron did not have some deep dark secret looming from his past. In fact, Leslie went on to share that Ron used to have hair down to his shoulders, and played in a rock band that traveled throughout the Midwest.

I was astounded that this business professional was once a rock and roll musician! I gave a big smile and said: "Ronnie, you have been holding out on me! It is time to 'get the ball rolling' with a praise band at the church!" Believe me, I was very excited to discover this hidden talent in our congregation. Not to mention, he is a long-standing deacon, so I knew we could quickly gain some leadership momentum on this new adventure.

I also realized that addressing this issue was going to "ruffle some feathers" in the church. I knew that some well-meaning people would possibly get their feelings hurt, and take the decision to change our style of music as a personal attack. This was not our intention, but anytime you make changes, it is going to have an adverse effect with some. Quite frankly, significant changes usually result in a few people leaving the church. As I have often said, anytime the train leaves the station, not everybody gets on board. That is a reality of ministry.

However, I firmly believe that the mission of reaching people for Christ is bigger than our feelings and personal preferences. Therefore, we eventually made the change and never looked back. The vast majority of our congregation embraced the new music with great enthusiasm. In fact, it reminded me of the movie "Sister Act" when an "enlightened Nun" brought contemporary music to the church. As a result of the change, our music has helped us go to the next level of ministry. Our Positive Faith Praise Band and singers are a tremendously talented ministry team with a heart for worship. They always do a great job of "setting the table" for the pastor to serve the "Bread of Life."

I firmly believe that the mission of reaching people for Christ is bigger than our feelings and personal preferences.

Our change of musical style has also helped us reach a new type of positive church transfer. There are many people in the "seeker movement" who like the music of their church, but have grown hungry for the Word of God. They have come to realize that cotton candy is sweet, but you cannot live on it. When they visit New Life, they enjoy our music, and often find what they have been "searching for" concerning the scriptural message.

The main idea concerning "facing the music" is the concept of being primarily contemporary in this area of ministry. This still allows plenty of "breathing room" to incorporate some foundational hymns. After all, there are some modern arrangements of some of the great hymns of the faith that are outstanding. I think it is wise to include one each week. It can pay rich dividends toward building a bridge between the young and the old, and help reduce a generational divide in the church.

Overall, our evolution toward a more contemporary style of Christian music has been very positive for New Life. It has been an outstanding blessing to many believers, and helped us reach some unbelievers with the life-changing power of the gospel. I would encourage anyone to "face the music" and make any necessary adjustments to improve this vital aspect of ministry.

As the Scripture says in Psalm 150:3-6: *Praise Him with the sound of the trumpet; Praise Him with the lute and harp! Praise Him with tambourine and dancing; Praise Him with stringed instruments and flutes! Praise Him with loud cymbals; Praise Him with resounding cymbals! Let everything that has breath praise the Lord. Praise the Lord!* Sounds like an exciting worship service with a praise band to me!

CHAPTER 10

TEAM CHEMISTRY

A team will out perform a talented group of individuals. History has repeatedly reinforced that truth. The Dallas Mavericks won the 2011 NBA championship, once again proving the power of teamwork over individual talent. Miami boasted the talent of LeBron James, but team chemistry brought the title to Dallas. Team Chemistry enables people to harness the collective energy of the group, known as synergy.

One time, while coaching a little league all-star team, I had the opportunity to teach a young man the importance of team- *Team Chemistry enables* work. We had an outstanding *people to harness the collec-* group of ten year olds that won *tive energy of the group,* the district, and had moved on *known as synergy.* to the regional championship series. In the second inning, we fell behind by a score of 9-1. At the end of the inning, the boys dropped their heads as they slowly walked into the dugout.

I cheered them on and encouraged them to hustle off the field. The boys picked up the pace and sprinted off the field. All except Phil, who continued to walk off the diamond. I told Phil to hustle in, but he kept showing his defiance. I gave him one last opportunity to hustle, like everybody else. However, Phil thought that because he was our shortstop, and a key hitter as well, he did not need to listen to the coach.

When he finally made it to the dugout, he grabbed his bat because he thought it was his turn to hit. However, I told Phil that since he was "too tired" to hustle off the field, we would give him a rest on the bench. The look of shock on his face, and his teammates was priceless.

Next came Phil's Dad out of the bleachers. He wanted to know why his son was taken out of the game. He let me know that his son was the best player on the team. He even boldly declared that we could not win without Phil. I explained that whether we win or lose, our team would hustle on every play. His son was no exception.

He walked back to the bleachers in anger and disbelief. Then he announced for all to hear that: "the coach is an idiot!" It was an interesting moment at the little league ballpark. However, I wanted to teach championship character more than win a championship game. The other coaches were in agreement, and the game continued.

However, Disney could not have scripted the finish any better if they tried. In the final inning, we still trailed 9-1. Then the boys started a rally, and the momentum began to shift. Soon the score was 9-7 with two outs, and runners on second and third. I called time, and held a meeting with the assistant coaches. I smiled and told them that I believed Phil had learned his character lesson. They all whole-heartedly agreed.

I stuck my head in the dugout and asked Phil if he was ready to play ball. He said, "Yes sir!" I announced to the umpire that Phil was coming back into the game, and he was due to bat. He grabbed a bat and sprinted to the plate. Phil crushed the first pitch for a line drive double up the gap! Both runs scored and the game was tied. The next batter got a base hit and Phil scored the winning run! The team went wild with enthusiasm!

After the game, Phil's mother approached me. I thought to myself, here we go again. However, she thanked me for teaching her son teamwork, and respect for authority. She was truly grateful that we were teaching championship character.

Incidentally, Phil never caused another problem as we went on to finish 8th in the state. I also had the opportunity to coach him two years later on another all-star team. It was a joy to watch Phil develop into a role model of respect, teamwork, and hustle. They also won the district, and finished State Runner-Up. Most importantly, the boys learned the value of working together for a common goal.

I believe a scriptural passage provides seven keys for building an effective team. The Bible says: *And we urge you, brethren, to recognize those who labor among you, and are over you in the Lord and admonish you, and to esteem them very highly in love for their work's sake. Be at peace among yourselves. Now we exhort you, brethren, warn those who are unruly, comfort the fainthearted, uphold the weak, be patient with all. See that no one renders evil for evil, to anyone, but always pursue what is good both for yourselves and for all* (I Thessalonians 5:12-15).

Leadership is the first key to team chemistry ("those who labor among you, and are over you in the Lord"). Everything rises and falls on leadership. It is true in business, politics, athletics,

Everything rises and falls on leadership.

the home, and certainly the church. People will seldom rise above the level of the leadership. Therefore, it is important to keep growing as a leader. Keep reading good books (starting with the Good Book), and surround yourself with positive people. The books we read and the people we associate with will have a significant impact on our growth as a leader.

As a ministry leader, consider yourself as a player coach. You are one of the players, but also a leadership coach. Participate in the work of the ministry, but do not try to do everything. Develop other leaders as well. Remember, every team needs a coach, but a professional team has an owner. In ministry, the owner is Jesus Christ.

It is also wise to lead like an architect, instead of a fireman. An architect is a designer, but a fireman is primarily a responder. The pastor that is constantly running around "putting out fires" will become frustrated in ministry. However, when you develop plans to carry out ministry goals, you will be more productive. In fact, some wise advance planning will keep many fires from even getting started.

Respect is the next key to team chemistry ("esteem them highly"). Respect is like a boomerang. What you send out is usually what will come back. Therefore, give respect and you will gain respect. To help reduce resentment toward leadership, it is always best to earn respect, instead of demanding it. Remember, a little respect can go a long way in developing positive relationships with those you are leading.

Unity is another key aspect of team chemistry ("be at peace among yourselves"). It is important to be unified in purpose. Everyone needs to be working for a common cause, and moving in the same direction. This includes being united in strategy.

After all, there are various ways to carry out a Great Commission ministry. However, to accomplish the power of synergy, it is important to "put your shoulder to the wheel" with the same strategy. Otherwise, the team will pull apart and fall apart. Never forget, united we stand, divided we fall. Refuse to allow the enemy to divide and conquer. Remain unified in spirit, and accomplish the mission with a common strategy.

Confrontation is another key to building team chemistry ("warn the unruly"). Success without conflict is unrealistic. The concept of "unruly" is an interesting word picture. It is a military term to describe someone that is breaking rank. It is the concept of "marching to your own drum beat." It includes the idea of ignoring the instruction of the leadership. This is very detrimental to team chemistry.

Therefore, sometimes people have to be confronted. When this is inevitable, try the "sandwich approach" to confrontation. Just like a sandwich has two slices of bread with some meat in the middle, begin and end your conversation on a positive note. Include the "meat" of the matter, but affirm the person at the beginning and end of the meeting. I have found this method to be a wise approach to conflict resolution.

However, on rare occasions, you may have to "cut bait" on talent. If someone refuses to listen, and continues to go their own way, you may have to let them walk away. Otherwise, you can lose the respect of other team players. This will have a crippling effect on your leadership in the long run. No one is indispensable in the Lord's work. Two thousand years of church history has proven that principle. The team mission of the Great Commission is bigger than individual talent.

Encouragement is also a key element in building team chemistry ("comfort the fainthearted, uphold the weak"). Encouragement is the partner of success. It is the ability to look for the good and find it. Encouragement is to inspire someone with hope. We need the inspiration of encouragement like we need oxygen to breath.

The team mission of the Great Commission is bigger than individual talent.

Be a hope builder and you will be like a magnet for the Lord. Be known for "patting people on the back" instead of "kicking them in the pants." Positive motivation produces confidence, which unleashes the faith to succeed. However, negative motivation produces resentment, and the fear of failure becomes the focus. Remember; hope builders are balcony dwellers that lift people up to a higher level of living.

Patience is another key element of team chemistry ("be patient with all). We have to learn to "put up" with one another on this journey of faith. Growth is a process, and the goal is progress not perfection. We need to keep in mind that it takes time to mature as a believer. Therefore, "cut a little slack" with those serving in ministry with you. We are human and mistakes are going to happen. The key is to "not trip over the same rock twice" as we learn from our shortcomings. As long as we are taking three steps forward for every two steps backward, we will achieve the goal of progress.

Love is the final aspect to keep in mind concerning team chemistry ("pursue what is good for yourselves and all"). Love is the ultimate badge of the believer. Love always takes the high road, and never takes the low road. Love is the glue that holds together all the other aspects we have covered concerning team chemistry.

Loving leadership will respect others and promotes team harmony. Love keeps the "care in your candor" when confrontation is necessary. Love encourages others with hope for the future, which produces power in the present. Love is the bond of believers, which produces patience with people. Bottom line, love always succeeds.

One final thought. Since team chemistry is such a powerful force, the devil wants to destroy it. After all, "a house divided against itself cannot stand." Therefore, the enemy will "stir the waters" to create dissension and disunity. His goal is to sidetrack the church from the mission of the Great Commission.

After serving at New Life for 16 years, I saw first hand the strategy of Satan to attempt to divide and conquer. We made the painful decision to dismiss a staff member. It was a necessary conclusion to a disappointing situation. Unfortunately, it became even more disappointing when a small pocket of people tried to create a large division. They began "sowing seeds of discord" and working the "rumor mill" with great precision.

I met with our leadership to give the situation prayerful and careful consideration. We decided to address the problem in a public setting. The church was packed the evening we held the meeting. We clearly stated the issue, and reviewed the mission and vision of the church. We challenged the people to "keep the main thing the main thing."

Then Ralph stood up and asked to speak. It was completely unexpected, and I had no idea what he wanted to say. However, I sensed the Lord's leading, so I "yielded the floor" to Ralph. He stated that he had seen this type of thing before, and it tears up churches. He shared his gratitude that New Life preaches God's Word, and focuses on the gospel. He went on to express his deep appreciation for me as pastor.

When Ralph finished speaking, the entire congregation rose to their feet in a thunderous applause. You could have "knocked me over with a feather" as I watched the scene unfold. It was one of the greatest defining moments in the history of the church. We never looked back as we united together, and marched forward by faith.

Incidentally, the small pocket of dissension "threw in the towel" and left the church. However, during the next twelve months we had a record year in baptisms! Over the next few years we successfully completed an expansion campaign entitled: pay for one; build another. We burned the mortgage, purchased more ground, and built our 862-seat worship stadium. God had pruned the vine, and restored our team chemistry for our Great Commission ministry.

My friend, never underestimate the power of team chemistry. It is the invisible inspiration that can take a team from good to great. Build it, and ignite your enthusiasm for your labor of love. Harness it, and increase your energy with the power of synergy. Team chemistry; capture it, and soar with your strengths for the glory of God!

CHAPTER 11

IT'S A FAMILY AFFAIR

Often times, in small churches, one family will eventually surface as the major influence of the church. It is not always by design, but it just seems to work out that way. Sometimes it is simply the natural result of one family that stuck it out through the years. Consequently, one characteristic that can surface is the "Patriarchal System" that is common in some extended families.

The "Patriarchal System" is an unspoken law that the oldest male of the extended family is the authoritative influence of the entire family. It is understood that everyone follows the lead of the patriarch. This tradition can run very deep, and "heaven help" the person that goes against it.

This can have a damaging affect on a small church that is under the influence of a patriarch. Very little happens in the church without his approval. He is in all actuality, the final decision maker for the church. This man can hold the church in the "palm of his hand" simply by exercising his influence with the family. This can become an extremely difficult obstacle for a church to overcome.

The problem tends to magnify as the church experiences some growth. The new people are not "under the spell" of the patriarchal influence. Consequently, the patriarch feels threatened, and may become more interested in protecting his own power than he is advancing the church. At some juncture, it usually comes to a boiling point in the church.

This creates a dynamic that goes beyond the gospel for members of the extended family of the patriarch. They may like the growth of the church, and even embrace the changes the pastor has made to help bring about the growth. However, if they stand against the patriarch, they risk his "cold shoulder" as he sends an emotional message of disapproval. If these family members continue to "swim against the tide" of the patriarch, he may eventually emotionally ostracize the renegade family members.

This creates a real dilemma for any family members that are excited about the growth of the church. They feel like they are caught between a "rock and a hard place" concerning their love for the church, and their relationship with their family patriarch. These family members know that the patriarch can "wield his power" with great skill as he controls the family and the church. Therefore, they nearly always choose to "play it safe" and follow his lead. There is just too much pressure to remain loyal to the family.

Tragically, the gospel gets put on the "back burner" and the patriarch keeps the small church under his complete control. Eventually, the new converts move on, and everything goes back to the way things were. The patriarch is pleased with the church, and he is proud of his family for sticking together. In time, the discouraged pastor also moves on, and the church begins their search for a new pastor. This process is repeated over and over again, and the gospel remains hidden behind the patriarchal system.

In order for a small church to break out of this holding pattern, the patriarch usually needs to be confronted. The timing for this type of courage is crucial. It is a "high stakes gamble" that will undoubtedly create "no small stir" in the church. Consequently, this is one "can of worms" that must be opened up very carefully. It is important to be "prayed up" when you walk into this "den of lions" because the roar

The purpose of the gospel is more important than the power of a patriarch.

will be heard all over the church. It is also important to keep in mind that the purpose of the gospel is more important than the power of a patriarch.

A good promise of scripture to claim as you tackle this problem is Isaiah 41:10. God says: *Fear not for I am with you; Be not dis-*

mayed, for I am your God. I will strengthen you. Yes I will help you. I will uphold you with my righteous right hand.

I will never forget the evening that I claimed that promise in my heart, while facing a showdown with the church patriarch. It was near the completion of my first year of service as pastor. The church had grown in Sunday morning worship attendance from 25 to 75. Most of our growth had come through evangelism, and the church had established some positive inroads with the community. However, even though it was an exciting time for the ministry, the patriarch had become upset. It all "came to a head" one evening during a meeting with the deacons. Let me explain.

There were five men who served as deacons and four of them were related to one another. They were good guys, but they just happened to be related. The deacons that I originally inherited were as follows: the patriarch, the son of the patriarch, the son-in-law of the patriarch, a man married to a granddaughter of the patriarch, and one non-family member. Obviously, the deacon body looked like a "family affair" to say the least.

Therefore, when an issue surfaced that involved the patriarch; I knew it would be a delicate situation. He had become upset over an issue and stopped attending church. It was his way of "sending a message" of disapproval. However, even though he was not attending our worship services, he still showed up to "wield his power" in a leadership setting.

Therefore, I ventured out where "angels fear to tread" in an attempt to resolve the conflict. Believe me, I aged ten years in twenty minutes, as the meeting unfolded after our opening prayer. I asked the patriarch to explain himself to the group concerning his decision to stop attending the church services over the past several weeks. He stated in "no uncertain terms" that it was "none of my business" whether or not he attended the church services. He went on to share that: "nobody, including the pastor, was going to tell him what to do" concerning his conduct as a deacon.

I decided to see what kind of "hand I had been dealt" and asked the rest of the deacons their opinion on the matter. I started with the man who was the son of the patriarch. This was a "defining moment" in his life and a "defining moment" for the church as well. I still remember his words as he said: "Daddy, I love you, but you are wrong on this one." He went on to ask his father to reconsider his attitude in the area of leadership. The rest of the men agreed.

The patriarch immediately resigned as a deacon. Surprisingly, he did attend the church fairly regularly over the next couple of years. However, we eventually outgrew the facilities, and sold the building to a start-up church. We purchased ground, and met in a temporary location, while making plans to build new facilities and relocate the church campus. During this time, his discomfort became noticeably evident once again.

He attended the first Sunday the church met in our temporary facilities, but never came back. I tried to shake his hand after the service, but he intentionally turned his back, and walked away from me. I also went to see him a few months later, but when he opened his front door and saw me standing there, he simply closed the door in my face.

A few years later, while he was on his deathbed, he even instructed the family to inform me that I was not welcome to attend his funeral. His deeply held grudge that he harbored against me was literally extended beyond the grave. Trust me on one thing, when you ruin the "family affair" of a patriarch, he never forgets.

Jesus *said: Do not think that I came to bring peace on earth. I did not come to bring peace but a sword...He who loves father or mother more than Me is not worthy of Me* (Matthew 10:34,37). The son of the patriarch experienced this challenge first hand. However, his biggest disappointment was the fact that his dad missed so many blessings that God has poured out on New Life.

Our ministry has been blessed for many reasons through the years. However, we would not be where we are today, if it had not been for the courage of a son to stand for the gospel, and experience the pain of standing up to his dad, the patriarch. I am very grateful to say that the son has stayed with the church all these years. In fact, I cannot think of anyone who has been more faithful and loyal to the New Life ministry. He remains a great friend of mine to this day, and he is an outstanding "role model" of a positive faith believer.

We have overcome many obstacles through the years, but this was definitely an important victory in the early years. It was a painful experience, but a profitable experience. It helped us take a major step toward moving away from a "family affair" and moving toward a community minded ministry. It required strong faith, great courage, a sense of timing, and tremendous help from the Lord. In the end, it is a beautiful tribute to the power of the Word of God, and the life-changing power of the gospel.

CHAPTER 12

CULTURAL WALLS THAT
LEAD TO CULTURE SHOCK

Walls keep some people in and some people out. Walls naturally separate and isolate. That is the simple reality of walls.
In churches, cultural walls keep the congregation safe within, and
the community securely locked out. The walls create a place of
refuge and escape. If someone scales the wall, it may lead to culture shock.

Culture shock is difficult
to describe, but easy to feel.
It begins with the uneasy
feeling of being out of place.

Culture shock is difficult to describe, but easy to feel.

Then leads to the uncomfortable feeling that you are in the wrong
place. Culture shock is like standing on the wrong side of the
Jericho wall, and sensing it is about to collapse on you. That is a
feeling that will not help people connect with the church.

Think of it this way. Suppose a group of missionaries went to
Germany to plant a church with the original goal of reaching the
German people. However, once they arrive, they visit the
American Embassy to see if any Americans are already living in
Germany. They meet some English speaking Americans and start
an English speaking church. They search the country high and low
to find as many English-speaking people as they possibly can.
Some of the people may be from Canada, Great Britain, or even
Australia, but they all have one thing in common, which is the
English language.

As they begin to gather for worship, they also create a very
friendly environment for fellowship. In fact, it gives them a sense

of comfort and security because of their commonality. They experience a "homeland feeling" and it helps ease the discomfort of living in a foreign land. However, it soon becomes an isolated group of people. In fact, they actually build an enormous "cultural wall" that naturally keeps them from connecting with the very people they intended to reach with the gospel.

In a similar way, this same mistake was often made while planting churches outside the Bible belt during the 1950's, 1960's, and 1970's. The churches were started with good intentions, but a natural cultural wall soon developed. Consequently, theses churches are struggling today to connect with their communities. Let me explain.

In the 1950's, 1960's, and the 1970's the factories were booming in the industrial sections of the country. Vast amounts of people moved north to work in the factories, steel mills, machine shops, etc. Jobs were abundant and workers were desperately needed. Therefore, many families moved together and settled in the same town where they found work. Often times they could even find work in the same factory.

For example, in the South Bend, Indiana area, thousands of jobs were available in the numerous factories. Many of these plants operated three shifts as men and women "worked on the line" day and night. In places like Gary, Indiana, the steel mills were operating "around the clock." Good paying jobs were abundant for people willing to work by the "sweat of their brow." This was true in industrial areas all over the country. It was a paradise for the "working man" or the "blue collar" worker.

Naturally, many industrial towns began to expand with the influx of people. New homes, schools and churches were built to accommodate the growing communities. Stores and other businesses also sprang up to meet the needs of the people. It was the good life and many enjoyed it.

However, in this process, many people were uprooted from their homeland. Therefore, they began gathering in places where they could keep their cultural heritage alive. The local church became a popular venue to fulfill this need. Many were deeply religious people, so gathering together for worship was only natural. In this process, many churches unknowingly built an enormous cultural wall. In fact, if someone from the community happened to visit the church, they usually experienced culture shock.

This was often the case with many Southern Baptist churches. The attraction to the church went beyond worship and fellowship. It also became a sub-culture of their traditional heritage. Consequently, a few southern transplants, that did not even have SBC roots, still chose a Southern Baptist church to maintain familiar fellowship.

In fact, if you had a license plate from a southern state, you were probably going to get invited to a Southern Baptist Church. As the people were out and about, they would often look for southern license plates. If they spotted one, they would usually track that person down and invite him or her to church.

In some cases, the church even functioned like a "local union hall" for the people. Someone could move to town and visit a Southern Baptist Church, and by the end of the day, they usually knew where to find a good paying job. Basically, the church just naturally became the local gathering place for transplanted people.

Eventually, because their common denominator was their cultural heritage, a "cultural wall" was built between the church and the community. This cultural wall went virtually unnoticed by the church because it reflected their cherished sub-culture. Consequently, if someone from the community visited the church, they seldom "fit in" and often felt like an outsider.

However, plenty of "familiar faces" kept moving to town, so these churches could still experience numerical growth. In fact, attendance would often reach 150-200 people. This was similar in size to the churches they grew up in, so everything seemed fine. Nobody even took notice of the cultural divide between the church and community.

However, during the 1980's, things had started to change. The factories that were once booming were beginning to slow down, shut down, and leave town. For example, in the greater South Bend area, thousands of jobs left town. Consequently, the entire economy has changed. The days of people graduating from high school and getting a job down at the plant are practically over. Today, they are more likely to get a job as a waiter/waitress, while working on their degree.

The effect of the changing economy on churches beyond the Bible belt is astounding. Today, many of the churches that were started in the 1950's, 60's, and 70's have experienced significant decline. Some have even shut down. Many of the former members have either moved away, or passed away. Unfortunately, the ones that remain are clinging to old their old ways.

Many of these churches are left with 20-25 people that are completely isolated from the community. Through the years, the church simply became disconnected from the community. These churches are gradually dying on the vine. The well-meaning people may desire to fix the problem, but often are not sure how, or where to start.

We experienced the problem of a cultural wall first hand when we arrived at the First Southern Baptist Church of Mishawaka, Indiana. Quite frankly, it was a very different feeling the first Sunday I preached at the church. It was not just the small size of the congregation at the time. There was something else, but I could not put my finger on it. It was like there was a "foreign feeling" in the air. This struck me as very unusual because I had lived in the area my entire life.

Then as we went home, I said to my wife, "Did you notice that everybody had a southern accent at church today?" She had made the same observation as well. I continued to "supply preach" and quickly discovered that the handful of people that made up the congregation at that time, were all from Alabama, Mississippi, and Tennessee. They were very gracious people and their "southern hospitality" certainly lived up to its reputation. However, I must admit that coming across this sub-culture in our town was a new discovery for me.

I was also surprised to hear the people talking about how they were living in the North. To me, and the people I knew growing up, our area is considered the Midwest. However, to the church, we were living in the North. In fact, it was not uncommon to hear someone from the church refer to "outsiders" as "Yankees" (I did not immediately tell them that I am a huge New York Yankee fan).

I also began sensing that a few members felt a tremendous need to remain loyal to their homeland. It was as if some still viewed themselves as "strangers in a foreign land." They were wonderful people, and we loved them dearly, but we did notice some cultural differences. Believe me, it we was very apparent that we had joined the ranks of those who cheered for the Alabama Crimson Tide, Ole Miss, and the Tennessee Volunteers. I wasn't quite sure that I should reveal my love for Notre Dame!

Incidentally, after I had served as pastor for a few years, Notre Dame went undefeated in football. Lou Holtz had successfully coached the Fighting Irish to a national championship. I was "on cloud nine" and my zeal spilled over into the sermon. However, one "dear saint of God" corrected me after the service for publicly sharing my sentiments for Notre Dame. It was a good opportunity for me to "live and learn" as a young pastor.

I mention a few of these things to simply point out that we sensed the cultural wall first hand. In fact, we went through a period of complete culture shock. I am not talk-

> *There was an obvious sub-culture, which created a feeling of "insiders" and "outsiders."*

ing about the culture shock someone may feel by moving to a new community. We had lived here for years. I am describing the culture shock we felt in the church. There was an obvious sub-culture, which created a feeling of "insiders" and "outsiders." It was clearly keeping the church disconnected and closed off from the community.

The culture shock that we experienced was difficult to describe, but easy to feel. That is the way culture shock works, it is hard to define, but easy to recognize. It is not simply feeling out of place; it has more to do with feeling you are in the wrong place.

Sometimes churches defend the uneasy feeling that others have toward their ministry in spiritual terms. They may speak of the "convicting work of the Holy Spirit" that causes discomfort. However, we must be careful not to confuse the "conviction of God" with the "culture shock" a visitor may feel from our sub-culture environment.

Don't get me wrong; I am not suggesting we should "water down" the gospel in order to make people feel more comfortable. I am simply suggesting that we take an honest look at any cultural wall that may hinder evangelism. We must evaluate the ministry, and see if we are requiring people to climb over a wall in order to hear the gospel. If so, those cultural walls must be torn down for the sake of the gospel.

Consider the progression of the problem. First, a sub-culture in the church will create a cultural wall that blocks out the community. This naturally keeps indigenous people out of the church, which prohibits developing local leaders for the church. Consequently, the church becomes more insolated, and isolated from the community. Through the years, the cultural wall becomes so thick; that it becomes nearly impossible to penetrate. This damages evangelism, and in time, destroys the church. Therefore, the problem must be addressed. Rest assured, the obstacle can also be overcome. We have seen God do it at New Life.

Years ago, it was very apparent that we had our work cut out for us in terms of helping the church reach the community. Consequently, we began taking some steps to help the church better identify with the community. It was crucial to begin "chipping away" at the cultural wall that clearly isolated the church from the community. Along the same line, we also started building some bridges of love to begin connecting the church to the community.

Believe me, we did not grow from a handful of people to a congregation of several hundred without tearing down a few walls. It also did not happen overnight. The church had spent several years building a thick cultural wall, and it took a few years to remove it. In the early days of the pastorate, I simply tried to reduce the culture shock for visitors. This proved to be a very important step in the right direction.

We continue to evaluate the ministry to reduce unnecessary culture shock for visitors. We examine to see if any cultural walls are rising, so we can remove them for the sake of evangelism. After all, reaching people for Christ is worth it. In fact, I believe it is time to echo the words of the late President Ronald Reagan: "Tear down that wall!"

CHAPTER 13

THINK LIKE A MISSIONARY

I will never forget my first lesson on cross-cultural communication. It happened purely by accident while I was attending Bible College in up-state New York. It was my first experience of living outside the Midwest. I was 21 years old, and far away from my familiar surroundings and comfortable culture. However, it proved to be a great opportunity to observe a few regional differences between various sections of the USA.

For example, where I come from, soda is referred to as "pop." As a result, that expression caused some confusion when I first arrived in up-state New York. I walked into a grocery store and asked the stock clerk: "Where is your pop?" He gave me a puzzled look and asked me to identify myself. This seemed a little unusual, but I went ahead and told him my name. Then I asked him again: "Where is your pop?" This time the stock clerk stared at me, and demanded to know the "real reason" I was in the store.

By now, I was starting to wonder about the business they were running, and why this guy was so paranoid about pop! However, I decided to give it one last "all-American try" and politely said: "I am not trying to cause any trouble, just tell me where your pop is, and I will be on my way." To my complete amazement, the stock clerk shouted in anger: "Why have you come in here looking for my pop? He does not even work here!"

Finally, I realized that he thought I was looking for his dad. You see, "pop" may have been my term for soda, but it was the stock clerk's term for his father. Once I understood the confusion, I further explained my request, and the problem was solved. He directed me to the "soda" aisle, and I purchased some "pop" to quench my thirst. Fortunately, that valuable lesson on cross-cultural communication went far beyond the grocery store that day. It also began to help me understand the value of thinking like a missionary in local church ministry.

When a missionary goes to the foreign field, they go through extensive preparation in order to better understand the process of cross-cultural communication. They study the language and the culture of the people they intend to reach with the gospel. The goal is to better equip them to understand the mindset of those in a particular foreign culture, in order to better communicate the gospel to them.

The initial training is just a start, and then the missionary must learn on the field. He or she observes the people and constantly makes adjustments along the way. Once they reach the field, they expand their understanding with a "live and learn" process. There is certainly a great deal of trial and error, but they always keep observing, learning, and improving.

Sometimes the missionary is fortunate enough to go where an experienced missionary is already serving. This provides a wonderful opportunity to be mentored by someone who "knows the ropes." It is important for the new missionary to listen and glean wisdom form the experienced laborer who has spent much time "paving the way." After all, if the jungle has already been cleared, you may not need your machete.

I believe the same type of training would be valuable for pastors and church planters serving in various regions of the United States as well. Anybody that thinks there are not cultural differences between various geographical regions in the United States of America is very mistaken. The Midwest is different from the South. The East Coast is different from the West Coast. Of course, it goes without saying that Texas is a world of its own!

One very important principle of a "missionary mindset" is to learn about the culture of the people they are seeking to reach. For example, a wise missionary does not proclaim the gospel to Germans through the language or lens of American culture. They learn to effectively communicate within the culture and minister accordingly. The same principle of cross-cultural communication is also needed for church planters in the USA.

Therefore, instead of passing out denominational literature in a door-to-door campaign, the pastor/church planter will want to explore ways to meet the people on their turf. It is always helpful to take the time to gain an understanding of the values, beliefs, and assumptions of the community. Looking at life through the world-view of those you are trying to reach will offer tremendous insight. It is very beneficial for discovering a starting point to dialogue about spiritual things.

It is always helpful to take the time to gain an understanding of the values, beliefs, and assumptions of the community.

Another crucial principle to keep in mind is the concept that perception is reality to the one doing the perceiving. Therefore, it is wise to evaluate your ministry, and eliminate needless negative perceptions that may hinder evangelism. For example, we discovered that in our area, the term "Southern Baptist" was conjuring up negative images in the minds of some people from our community. These false images were derived from old TV shows such as Hee Haw and the Beverly Hillbillies. Others even wondered if we belonged to the religious group known as the Snake Handlers.

Therefore, we removed the term "Southern Baptist" from our name. This was a strategic bridge building move to help us connect with our target audience. Our purpose was to remove a needless hurdle off the evangelism track. In a similar way, it would be foolish to call a church in the south "Yankee Baptist Church" for obvious reasons. I think you get the idea.

Another valuable principle of thinking like a missionary is the importance of learning the language of the targeted audience. Just as this is crucial when taking the gospel to a foreign country, the same principle is helpful for those who are crossing over into various regions of the USA. It is important to realize that some words have one meaning in one section of the country, but another meaning elsewhere.

The wise leader will be sensitive to eliminate certain expressions from their vocabulary to be more effective in cross-cultural communication. This is particularly important if an expression fuels a negative stereotype in the minds of your intended audience. After all, if a common expression from one cultural background creates a negative image in another culture, then it is worth making a change for the gospel.

It is also wise to seek honest feedback from someone indigenous to the community you are serving in. I chose to seek the advise from a successful business professional that I coached little league with for a number of years. We developed a personal friendship in the process, and began meeting for breakfast occasionally. Therefore, I felt comfortable enough to ask him a few exploratory questions to gain some insight from the non-churched community. The feedback was "worth its weight in gold." It definitely affirmed the principle that: perception is reality to the one perceiving it.

Perception is reality to the one perceiving it.

Never forget, certain expressions may have one meaning in one culture, but can be interpreted quite differently in another. Therefore, take an honest inventory of your vocabulary, and make sure your expressions do not reflect a different region of the country than where you are serving in ministry. After all, it does not make any sense to carelessly erect a cultural wall of separation from the very people you are trying to reach with the gospel.

I suggest taking a tip from national news broadcasters. They are very careful to work on their vocabulary and accent that appeals to the entire nation. Seldom, if ever, does a national news broadcaster have a dialect that connects them to any particular section of the country. With that in mind, it makes good sense, to evaluate our language for the sake of the gospel. Always remember, you never get a second chance to make a first impression.

It continually comes back to the all-important principle of thinking like a missionary. The wise missionary makes adjustments to their language and lifestyle in order to connect with another culture. They are more concerned about being sensitive to the people they want to reach with the gospel, instead of protecting their own cultural heritage. The constant goal is to remove walls, and build bridges for the gospel.

While we are on this subject, I also suggest using some discernment when your 'denominational big brother" is lending a helping hand. For example, a denominational mission team may volunteer to help canvass your neighborhood. The goal is positive, but the initial signal being sent to your community, may not connect with your targeted area. Therefore, I suggest doing your own outreach projects with the indigenous people from your community, who actively attend your church. In this process, no matter where you are serving, you will represent the community culture in which your church is located.

I also recommend that churches primarily use the mission teams for construction projects. The volunteer labor can be an outstanding asset, and help the church save tremendous money. It also creates a great opportunity to "whistle while you work" as you fellowship together with your denominational friends.

Another principle that is a good practice for those with a missionary mindset is to listen and learn from those who have done it, not those who may not even get it. It always amazes me that people will hang on every word of those who speak from theory, and ignore those who are actually in the trenches doing it. Therefore, talk to pastors who have reached indigenous people for Christ, helped them grow in faith, and trained them for leadership.

The seminary professors and denominational leaders have their place, but sometimes they have lost touch with the reality of the situation. For example, I was attending a meeting in Indianapolis, Indiana concerning the subject of revitalizing churches. At one point, the "denominational expert" made reference to us being in "Yankee land." It was very apparent to me that he was completely out of touch with the mindset of the Midwest, as he conducted a seminar for pastors in the Midwest.

Therefore, it is simply a wise practice to learn from people who have gone through the "school of hard knocks." There is much to glean from those who have "earned their stripes" the old-fashioned way, through trial and error. People who know what it means to "keep their hand to the plow and not look back" have a wealth of wisdom to offer. I think it is wise to "pick their brains" whenever possible. Therefore, I suggest taking every opportunity to gain valuable insight from those who have "blazed the trail" before us.

I close with an example that is not intended to be critical or condescending. I simply share it because it captures the content of this chapter. I hope you understand the loving spirit behind what I have to say on this subject of thinking like a missionary.

When I began writing this book, my wife and I took a Sunday, and randomly visited a small church in the Midwest. The friendly congregation had approximately 50 people in attendance. The pastor shared his good intentions of reaching their community, and presented a potential youth pastor for consideration.

During the service, they conducted the public interview of the young man being considered for the youth pastor. It was a great Sunday to observe this church in action. It was obvious to me that the Lord had directed our path to visit the church that day. The church was only a short distance from the home of my business professional friend that I spoke of earlier in this chapter. He had recently moved his family to a beautiful lake-home near this particular church. Therefore, I thought it would be interesting to see how well the church identified with their surrounding community.

The pastor explained that the youth pastor candidate had visited the church while serving on a mission team. Then the pastor gave several reasons why he believed the young man would make a good youth pastor for the church. Finally, he told the church that the young man was a "true son of the South." The people smiled and nodded in agreement with obvious approval.

Next, the young man opened the "good book" and preached a good sermon. However, I could not help but notice that he repeatedly used common southern phrases. It was very apparent that the congregation became endeared to the young man who spoke their language, and understood their culture. Unfortunately, it was not the language or the culture of their community. It reflected the cultural wall that had been built, which was keeping the local community out of that church.

My wife and I drove away with many memories of what our church was like many years ago. We were reminded of the incredible labor of love that it took to help our church connect with our community. It also solidified in my mind the importance of thinking like a missionary in order to communicate the gospel in an effective way.

I cannot emphasize enough the importance of the bridge building principle of: *becoming all things to all people that we might by all means win some* (I Corinthians 9:22). It provided insight for the original missionary, the Apostle Paul, as he developed cross-cultural communication to reach people for Christ. It will also help us learn to think like a missionary, and effectively reach our communities for Christ.

CHAPTER 14

HEART AND SOUL OF THE MATTER

There were only seventeen people sitting in the church auditorium "seeking the Lord's will" concerning asking me to serve as the next pastor. The church had been in existence for thirty years at that time, yet only seventeen adults remained. If you did the math, it really did not stack up very well for the church. They had also gone through twelve previous pastors during the same thirty-year period. That literally breaks down to changing pastors every two and half years. The math on this situation certainly did not "lean in my favor" in terms of building a lengthy ministry.

I fielded a variety of questions during the public interview. First, they asked if I believed in and practiced tithing. I told the group that from the moment of my conversion, I had gladly given a minimum of one-tenth of my income to the local church. I have always believed that when God gets your heart, He also gets your checkbook.

Cindi and I are also in total agreement concerning the biblical principle of tithing. We believe it is the starting blocks of biblical stewardship, but certainly not intended to be the finish line of Christian generosity. We truly enjoy this aspect of faith and are always amazed at God's faithfulness to us.

Next, I was asked if I would support world missions through the cooperative program of the SBC. This was another easy principle to affirm. After all, it makes sense to embrace the value of working together for world missions. The cooperative program is a great way to obey the Lord's command of taking the gospel to the entire world. It relieves the burden of missionaries raising their financial support, and allows them the opportunity to focus on the task of evangelism.

They also asked if I believe the Bible is the divinely inspired Word of God. I was very glad this question was included. It helped assure me that they wanted to build the ministry on the right foundation. I was happy to affirm my unwavering confidence in all of Scripture from Genesis 1:1 through Revelation 22:21. Through the course of the interview, other questions were asked, and I answered them to their satisfaction.

However, before they voted on me, I had two key questions of my own. These crucial questions would determine whether or not I wanted to serve as their pastor. The first question was simply this: Are you willing to do whatever is necessary to reach people with the gospel? I respectfully explained that we had to accept the fact that whatever they had been doing simply was not working. After all, the church had been in existence for thirty years, and now only seventeen adult members were sitting in a room, trying to determine if they wanted me as their pastor.

It was obvious that some changes would need to be made in order to become more effective in reaching people for Christ. I stated that the Great Commission would be our mission. I also tried to help them understand that the mission never changes, but sometimes our methods need to change. It was also made crystal clear that I believed the gospel was for all people. Therefore, anyone who responded to faith in Christ, and followed the Lord in baptism, would be welcome as a member.

The other question I asked was this: Who is going to lead? At

At that time the church had more committees than it had people!

that time the church had more committees than it had people! I explained my understanding of pastoral leadership based on I Peter 5:1-5. Christ is the Chief Shepherd, and the pastor is the under-shepherd of the Chief Shepherd. I agree with men like the late Dr. W.A. Criswell who taught that the three words used for leadership in that passage all refer to the office of the pastor. They differ only in function.

I explained to the people that God had called me to preach, and God had created me to be a leader. If they wanted pastoral leadership, then call me as their pastor. However, if they did not want pastoral leadership, then they would want to call someone else to serve as their pastor. I wanted to lead the church in a Great Commission ministry. It was really that simple.

I truly believe those two questions I asked the congregation that day are the "heart and soul" of ministry. It strikes at the very essence of our purpose as a church, and the essential responsibility of leadership. It "sets the table" to focus on the right priority, and "cuts through the red tape" of a committee structured church.

Roy, a deacon, responded that he wanted the pastor to lead the church. He also stated that he hoped we had to "push the walls out" of the church, as we reached people for Christ. That satisfied me. The vote was taken, and I received seventeen unanimous votes to become the thirteenth pastor of the church. However, only time would tell whether the number thirteen would be "unlucky" or the "magic" number for the congregation.

Our commitment to evangelism and pastoral leadership were put to the test in very first month. The first people that trusted Christ after I accepted the pastorate were an interracial couple. The husband was African-American and the wife was Caucasian. It became an initial defining moment in the ministry.

A few of the members had deep-rooted feelings concerning racial issues. In fact, one couple had "warned the church" that it would cease to be a segregated congregation if I became the pastor. I was unaware of this "warning" when the church called me as pastor, but it was soon drawn to my attention. I guess this particular couple had become very upset concerning a sermon I preached during the interim period. The theme of the message focused on taking the gospel to everyone.

I believe that John 3:16 is the very heart and soul of the New Testament. Jesus said: *For God so loved the world that He gave His only begotten Son, that whoever believes in Him should not perish but have everlasting life.* Therefore, based on the love of

God for all people, the application was made for the church to share the gospel with everyone in the community. It also meant that anyone that trusted Christ, regardless of his or her race, would be welcome as a member.

Unfortunately, the message made one couple very angry. Incidentally, they did not even bother to attend the congregational meeting when the church called me as pastor. However, they decided to "burn up the phone lines" once they "caught wind" that we baptized an interracial couple.

Therefore, I decided to visit the couple and seek to resolve the conflict. So I "put on my bullet proof vest" (figuratively speaking) and took Harold, a faithful deacon with me. Believe me, I was "getting an education" as a young pastor. I braced myself and rang their doorbell. I literally had no idea what was about to take place.

For the next several minutes, I felt like we stepped into a time machine, and went back to 1955 instead of 1985. It was an ugly scene. The prejudice feelings poured out of an angry and bitter heart. Eventually, the woman said, "I guess I do not sound very Christian do I?" Since she finally said something I could agree with, I politely affirmed her statement of not sounding very Christian.

I also tried to review the concept of John 3:16 concerning God's love for all people. However, the couple was unmoved concerning their attitude that "blacks and whites" do not need to worship together. I asked them what they planned on doing in heaven? It seemed like a reasonable question to me, but it only annoyed them.

Finally, after getting nowhere in this futile effort, I graciously explained that the decision was up to them. They could either adjust their attitude and worship with us, or find another church that shared their point of view. However, a new direction had been taken, and the good news of God's love was available to everyone. Incidentally, we never saw that couple in church again.

When Harold and I got in the car, I turned and asked him this question: "Well, brother, what did you think of that?" He responded: "Brother that kind of attitude has needed to be dealt with in this church for a long time." He also thanked me for my courageous stand for the gospel. We drove away and never looked back.

By the way, I am very pleased to report that the rest of the church fully accepted the interracial couple. The congregation welcomed them with "open arms" in a loving spirit of unity. It was a beautiful display of the love of Christ, and the gospel went forward in the power of the Holy Spirit.

I am convinced that God tested the congregation very early in my pastorate. If we had failed that test, we undoubtedly would not have experienced the blessing of God through the years. After all, it is difficult to share the love of the Savior, if you reject people based on the color of their skin. I believe that God "removed a roadblock" for the sake of the gospel. The Lord "pruned the vine" and "paved the way" to bless our future.

Fortunately, not every roadblock to evangelism has been that dramatic by any means. However, any roadblock to the life-changing gospel is damaging to the mission. Therefore, it is important to do some "soul searching" from time to time, and deal with any unhealthy attitudes or unproductive actions.

Sometimes, changes need to be made for the sake of the gospel such as: replacing an outdated program, eliminating an ineffective method, shifting the style of music, or even redirecting a ministry volunteer. Basically, we must be willing to sacrifice any "sacred cow" on the altar of the Great Commission.

Through the years, our methods have adjusted many times, but the mission has always remained the same. Our constant goal is to be guided by the Great Commission. It helped us focus on the heart and soul *Through the years, our methods have adjusted many times, but the mission has always remained the same.*

of ministry in the early days, and has kept us on track through the years. It has also helped us "push the walls out" several times.

I believe that any congregation that is faithful to the mission, and flexible for the mission; will be fruitful in the mission. Yes, when loving Christians reach out with the love of Christ, the love of God will bless your ministry.   It truly is the "heart and soul" of the matter.

CHAPTER 15

ROBERT HAS "NO BUSINESS" RULING

When I was coaching little league, I really enjoyed the opportunity to have a positive influence in the community. Along with teaching the game of baseball, we taught about "championship character" to help develop winners in the game of life. It was a rewarding experience to be involved in a "front-line ministry" opportunity. We kept it fun for the ballplayers, built confidence in the team, and won a few games in the process. Most importantly, we developed lasting friendships with many families. Those relationships have "opened many doors" for the gospel, and God, continues to bless those "open doors" today.

However, I also met a few unique people during my coaching days as well. There was a handful of people that seemed to find their "great meaning in life" by making the decisions for the ballpark. They would sit around for hours and discuss obvious decisions that could easily have been made in a matter of minutes. It seemed to give them a real a sense of significance as they "ran the show" and made the decision concerning the amount of popcorn to have ready for opening day!

It seemed like a few of those people had "no other life" than the "small life" they lived at the ballpark. Believe me, some of those folks really needed to "get a life" outside of little league. Don't get me wrong; they were good people that simply had a bad habit of making "mountains out of molehills" in the decision making process.

Unfortunately, I have met some of these same types of people in the church. They tend to be the ones that know very much about "Roberts Rules of Order" and know very little of what the Bible has to say about biblical leadership. They sit around and scrutinize everything as they challenge the authority of nearly every decision.

Think about it. What did the church do for two thousand years before Robert wrote his book on the rules of order? Don't you suppose the church got along okay the first two thousand years by following the New Testament? Don't you think that God gave leadership qualifications in I Timothy 3:1-7; Titus 1:5-9; and I Peter 5:1-5 for a reason? Can you imagine the early church "ruling out of order" leaders such as Peter, Paul, Barnabas, and James as they gave direction to the church as recorded in Acts 15?

Sadly, I think some of our believing friends think that someone stood up in that meeting and directed the future of the church by saying: "I have seen a vision and a new inspired text is coming on the horizon by which all churches will be governed. Soon the New Testament will be obsolete when it comes to biblical leadership in the local church. Therefore, I am sorry to inform you that we have heard too much already from Peter, Paul, Barnabas, and James. Consequently, I am 'ruling them out of order' from any further discussion. After all, it will be out of order in the future, so we might as well rule them out of order today."

That type of thinking would have been ridiculous then, and it is just as foolish today. The Bible does not even remotely suggest that the church is a "free for all" in the area of leadership. Everything rises and falls on leadership, and the church desperately needs biblical leadership to "stay on course" of a Great Commission ministry. Trust me, "keeping the main the main thing" does not just naturally happen. It requires pastoral courage to accept his God-given leadership role.

The Greek New Testament uses three words to describe the role of the pastor. The word *poimen* emphasizes the role of the pastor as the shepherd who leads in spiritual ministry. The word *episkopos* emphasizes the administrative responsibilities of the pastor as he provides general oversight of the ministry. The word *presbuteros* emphasizes the importance of spiritual maturity needed in pastoral ministry. All three words are used interchangeably in First

Peter 5:1-5 concerning the role of the pastor. They differ only in the emphasis of function.

It has been my observation through the years that most congregations accept the biblical teaching concerning the pastor as a shepherd (poimen), and a spiritually mature believer (presbuteros). However, some congregations struggle with the idea of the pastor serving in the role of an overseer/administrator (episkopos). Some people strongly resist the concept of authority that God has granted to the position of the pastor. However, most thriving churches embrace the concept of authoritative pastoral leadership. Healthy churches give the pastor the freedom to lead, and they do not plot the next "mutiny on the bounty" in the process.

This also works very well in our busy culture. Time has become the number one commodity with many people today. The modern family has a jam-packed schedule of work, school functions, and extra-curricular activities of every kind. They are "on the go" like never before. Concerning the church, they are interested in worship, Bible study and prayer, effective programming, connecting with a community of believers, and "front-line ministry" opportunities to reach unbelievers.

The modern family expects competent pastoral leadership and they are glad to find it. They resent meetings that waste their time, and they will not participate in such futility. Supportive people consider it ridiculous for the church to be held hostage by a few "old-timers" who know how to use "Roberts Rules of Order" to their advantage. Thinking people are turned off to any church that resembles a new version of the old Mickey Mouse Club. Make no mistake about it; the modern *Trust me, "keeping the main the main thing" does not just naturally happen.* family is looking for a church with an effective ministry and visionary leadership.

This hunger for leadership is a tremendous opportunity for the wise pastor. It is a great time to step forward and fill the leadership vacuum of the church. Assemble a leadership team to "brainstorm with you" to develop more effective ways to reach your community for Christ. Equip some godly men to serve as deacons, and to assist the pastor by "putting their shoulder to the wheel" in servant ministry. Don't be afraid to "cut through all the red tape" that is hindering the work for the Lord. Bottom line, have the courage to get "Robert out of the way" of a Great Commission Ministry!

Unfortunately, some "small-minded believers" would rather get rid of a Great Commission Pastor, and keep "their church" under their control. I know of one situation where a group of immature deacons plotted against the pastor and planned his demise. They met behind the scenes and "set the strategy" to remove their pastor in a way that would be unacceptable in the world, and a completely unthinkable in the church. The actions of the thoughtless deacons were an absolute embarrassment to the Christian faith.

Healthy churches give the pastor the freedom to lead, and they do not plot the next "mutiny on the bounty" in the process.

The church followed the "leadership" of the deacons, and "Roberts Rules of Order" to successfully accomplish their heartless plan. The congregation voted out their Bible teaching pastor who stood for the Word of God. While they were at it, they decided to vote out the youth pastor, who had recently led thirty students to Christ. It was a real "two for one bargain" as the congregation rebelled against pastoral leadership.

Sadly, because they followed *Roberts Rules of Order* they foolishly believed that everything was done *decently and in order* (I Corinthians 14:40). Simply because they knew how to manipulate a system, they were convinced they had done the will of God. Meanwhile, God-given leadership was grossly mistreated, and the name of Christ was dragged through the mud.

I wish I could say that this is an isolated incident. However, it tragically goes on all too often in churches that are more interested in "following Robert" than they are following Christ. Make no mistake about it, "Robert has no business ruling" the church.

Following *Roberts Rules of Order* might be okay for the Little League Park, but thriving churches have learned to get "Robert out of the way" to allow the Great Commission to lead the way.

CHAPTER 16

KEEP THE GOOD NEWS, GOOD NEWS

People smile when they share good news. Whether it is the announcement of the birth of a child, a promotion at work, winning the big game, graduating from college, being chosen for a part in the school play, or a host of other exciting events, people love

People smile when they share good news.

sharing good news. The excitement is "written on our face" as we speak of some positive event in our life. The same should be true when we share the good news of the gospel.

I have experienced the joy of seeing many people of all ages trust Christ as their personal Savior. For example, recently I had the privilege of leading a 94-year-old man to personal faith in Christ. His wife is a faithful listener to our Power for Living radio broadcast, and my oldest son just happens to be married to their granddaughter. Therefore, we had a positive contact from which to build a bridge for the gospel.

This particular man was raised in a formal religion, but lacked a personal relationship with Christ. It was a joy to visit him, and find some common ground, and share the good news of the gospel. He was a very quiet man, and kept to himself. However, he had expressed to a family member that he was afraid to die.

Therefore, we visited him and looked for an opportunity to share the good news of the gospel. At one point, I asked Him if I could share some promises of Christ in the New Testament that could be an encouragement to Him. He agreed and I started with John 3:16 and kept going from there. Eventually, I asked Him if he would like to invite Christ into His life. I also explained the prayer of faith that would help him trust Christ as Savior. He bowed his head, and verbally prayed to invite Christ into his life. It was thrilling!

Later, as we left, the elderly gentlemen stood at the picture window, and smiled from ear to ear, waving goodbye. I was told that he had not expressed that type of joy in years. My oldest son was with me and we rejoiced all the way back to the church. Once again, it confirmed that it is a joy to share the good news of the gospel, and it is a joy for people who receive the good news. Whether someone is 94 years young, or only four years old, or anywhere in between, the same gospel will draw people to faith in Christ.

In the simplest sense, the gospel means good news. The best news in the world is the truth that: God left heaven in the person of Jesus Christ, was born of a virgin, lived a sinless life, went to the cross and died a sacrificial death for our sins, and bodily rose again the third day.

The fact that Jesus conquered sin, death, and hell itself, is truly good news. The opportunity for all of humanity to experience the forgiveness of sins, and personal salvation through faith in Jesus Christ, truly is the best news in the world. Therefore, it should be shared in a positive way, and joyfully announced to all people.

This truth is well stated in Luke 2:10-11 when the angel said to the shepherds: *I bring you good tidings of great joy which will be to all people. For there is born to you this day in the city of David a Savior, who is Christ the Lord.* Yes, the gospel is good news. Therefore, it should be shared with a smile, and in a spirit of joy.

Jesus said that followers of Him would become fishers of men (Matthew 4:19). This includes information and intent. The information that people need is the good news of the death, burial, and resurrection of Christ for our sins (I Corinthians 15:3-4). Fishing also includes a goal of catching fish. Therefore, the intent of evangelism is to help people place their faith in Christ, or "win them to Christ"(Proverbs 11:30, I Corinthians 9:22). Since we are sharing the good news of Jesus Christ; it is a good idea to keep the good news, good news.

One good way to start a gospel presentation on a positive note is to begin with John 3:16, which says: *For God so loved the world that He gave His only begotten Son, that whoever believes in Him should not perish but have everlasting life.* It is exciting to explain the "gospel in a nutshell" based on the truth that God loves all people. In fact, we can all place our own name in place of the word "world" in John 3:16.

It is also good to follow up with John 3:17, which says: *For God did not send His Son into the world to condemn the world, but that* **It is powerful to explain the** *the world through Him might be* **fact that God is not out to** *saved.* It is powerful to explain **make your life miserable.** the fact that God is not out to make your life miserable. He offers a life of meaning, fulfillment, and satisfaction. That is the essence of the abundant life that Jesus spoke of in John 10:10.

Next it is valuable to read I John 5:12-13, which says: *He who has the Son has life; he who does not have the Son of God does not have life. These things are written to you who believe in the Son of God, that you may know that you have eternal life, and that you may continue to believe in the name of the Son of God.*

At this point it is very positive to point out that God wants people to know for sure where they will spend eternity. This leads us to the "million dollar question." How do we receive Jesus Christ into our life? After all, some churches may say it happens at baptism, or another church may teach that it happens during communion. Others may teach that we simply need to be kind to our neighbor, and follow the Golden Rule. However, the most important key to keep in mind is: What does the New Testament teach about receiving Christ into our life?

This leads us to the value of understanding the reason we need Christ in our life. Romans 3:23 says: *"For all have sinned and fall short of the glory of God."* Sin in the New Testament means a couple of things. First it means to "miss the mark" or "fall short of the standard." The problem is we often compare ourselves to the wrong standard. We might look around and decide that we are just as good as anyone else. This may be true, but other people are not the standard. You see, Christ is referred to as the "glory of God" in John 1:14, which makes Him the correct standard. Therefore, when we compare ourselves to Jesus, we discover there is "room for improvement" for all of us.

I like to explain it this way. Suppose two people stood on the bank of the Mississippi river, and each tried to jump across to the other side. One person may leap further than the other, but both fall way short, and end up being swept down the river. The same is true with sin. Humanly speaking, one person may not seem as bad as someone else, but without Christ, we are all helplessly headed for the wrong destination.

The other definition for sin is found in I John 3:4, which says: *"Whoever commits sin also commits lawlessness, and sin is lawlessness.* Bottom line, it is a sin to violate any or all of the Ten Commandments. Basically, an easy way to think of sin is in the spelling of sin. The problem is the "I" in the middle. God tells us to do one thing, but "I" decide to do my own thing. Consequently, we sin against God, by breaking His law.

The other problem with sin is explained in James 2:10, which says: *For whoever shall keep the whole law, and yet stumble in one point, he is guilty of all.* The problem is that the moral law of God is like a chain. When one link breaks, the entire chain collapses. Therefore, our relationship with God has been broken because no one can honestly say they have kept all of the Ten Commandments their whole life. Jesus further defined our problem when He taught that it is not just the act of sin, but also the attitude underneath it.

The result of our sin is separation from God. Romans 6:23 says: *For the wages of sin is death, but the gift of God is eternal life in Christ Jesus our Lord.* Death results in separation. In physical death, the soul is separated from the body. In spiritual death, the soul is separated from God. Therefore, we need a bridge to connect us to God.

That is exactly what Jesus did on the cross. He bridged the gap between humanity and God. Therefore, He made it possible for humanity to reconnect to God through faith in Jesus Christ. Romans 5:8 says: "But God demonstrates His own love toward us, in that while we were still sinners, Christ died for us." Jesus has done for us what we could never do for ourselves.

The concept of salvation by faith in Christ is reinforced in Ephesians 2:8-9, which says: *For by grace you have been saved through faith, and that not of yourselves; it is the gift of God, not of works, lest anyone should boast.* If we could earn our own salvation by the good things we do, then we would have a big bragging party in heaven. However, the Scriptures are clear, the only person we will brag about in heaven is Jesus. Grace means an undeserved favor, which is why we owe it all to Jesus Christ.

Faith in the New Testament means the acceptance of the facts, and personal trust. Therefore, it is important to believe the good news of the death, burial, and resurrection of Christ for our sins. It is also important to apply our faith in Christ by personally trusting in Him for salvation. Romans 10:9-10 says: *That if you confess with your mouth the Lord Jesus and believe in your heart that God has raised Him from the dead, you will be saved.* For with the heart one believes to righteousness, and with the mouth confession is made to salvation. Romans 10:13 goes on to proclaim: *For whoever calls upon the name of the Lord shall be saved.*

The good news includes the fact that we never get a busy signal when we call on Christ for salvation. He always "answers the phone" when someone calls Him up in prayer. He promises to give eternal life to all who place their trust in Him for salvation.

I also like to illustrate personal faith in Christ with a simple chair. A person can know all about the chair. Where it was manufactured, and the type of material used to build the chair. They can fully believe that the chair will hold them up when they sit down. However, they have not completely trusted the chair until they sit down in it.

The same is true about the gospel of Jesus Christ. We can know all about the facts of the gospel. However, we have not truly believed in Christ until we have personally trusted Him as Savior and Lord. That is the very concept described in John 1:12 as "believing in and receiving Christ" into our life by faith.

It is also worth noting that sometimes people of great faith can experience some doubts about their salvation. When this occurs, it is wise to simply "take them back to the cross." I have seen this many times through the years. Occasionally, a believer just needs a little "blessed assurance" that "Jesus is mine."

I experienced this first hand with my brother Denny, shortly before he went home to be with the Lord. He had trusted Christ as a child during a revival service, and lived for Christ for many years. However, as he lay on his deathbed, some nagging doubts began to haunt him. One evening, Denny opened up and shared his concerns with me. Therefore, I reviewed the good news of the gospel, and the finished work of Christ on the cross. I asked Denny if he would like to reaffirm his faith in Christ. He said: "Mike, I think that is where I am."

I had the tremendous privilege of leading my dying brother in a simple prayer of faith in Jesus Christ. Denny poured out his heart to God in a humble expression of total trust in Christ. When he finished, he said: "I feel like the weight of the world is off my shoulders." Then he turned to his wife and said: "Marcia, I am ready to go be with Jesus." It is a moment that I will cherish for the rest of my life.

Denny also gave me permission to tell his story anytime I thought it might help others reaffirm their faith in Christ. On Sunday, August 15, 2010, the day after I helped conduct his funeral, I told Denny's story at New Life. We experienced an "unscheduled revival" as the Holy Spirit literally "high jacked" our service. During the invitation, we had to ask for additional counselors, as over 50 people publicly trusted Christ.

One couple visited for the first time from several miles away. They had not planned on attending; they were simply driving past New Life to visit family. However, they felt "strangely compelled" to pull into our parking lot and attend New Life. As a result, they were both gloriously saved that morning!

My friend, that is the power of the gospel! It is the good news that Jesus saves. Christ forgives us of our sins, provides a better way to live on earth, and takes us to heaven when we die. Therefore, share the gospel with a smile, and keep the good news, good news!

CHAPTER 17

RELIGIOUS RESPECT AND CULTURAL SENSITIVITY

When it comes to religious respect; I prefer the guiding principle of: *In the essentials unity, in the non-essentials liberty, in all things charity.* When it comes to cultural sensitivity; I am reminded of the little humorous story concerning some Christians in France attending a Bible study. It seems their discussion shifted to the subject of Christianity in America. They were appalled to discover that some "so-called Christians" in the United States actually smoked cigarettes. This so enraged these French believers that they jumped up and tripped over their wine glasses!

In a culture that places a high premium on tolerance and a low premium on truth, it is helpful to demonstrate a little "religious respect" for others. We must understand the "dangerous landmine" that we are walking through today. One thoughtless comment can ruin an opportunity to reach a lost person. The gospel may offend someone, but be careful not to communicate it in an offensive way. Never mistake rudeness for boldness.

I want to offer a couple of suggestions for people serving in ministry Beyond the Bible Belt. First in the area of baptism by immersion, it is sometimes wise to help the new believer make a self-discovery. This is particularly helpful for people who come to Christ from Catholic backgrounds because they can be sensitive about their religious roots. They often attach a strong family value to things such as: infant baptism, first communion, and confirmation. These events are often accompanied with a festive celebration with extended family and close friends.

Therefore, it usually takes some time for them to embrace the biblical mode of baptism by immersion. They may feel like they are betraying their upbringing and dishonoring their parents. Consequently, it is best for them to come to a "self-discovery" of baptism by immersion. I often begin their journey of faith by suggesting to the new believer to read the Gospel of John (one chapter a day for three weeks and they can read the entire Gospel). This will strengthen their faith (John 20:31).

Next I will suggest that they read through the book of Acts (one chapter a day for four weeks and they can read it through). I also ask them to make a note of who gets baptized and when they are baptized. Then we get together and talk about it. If they have followed the suggested reading plan, they have been reading their Bible for nearly two months. Lord willing, they have been attending church during the process as well.

As a result of their new spiritual journey, they have become more sensitive to spiritual truth. Consequently, during the follow-up conversation, I simply ask them what new insights they have gained in the area of baptism. On nearly every occasion, they have made a "self-discovery" concerning baptism by immersion, and they are usually ready to follow the command. It takes a little more time, but it is worth the wait. Their "believer's baptism" becomes a beautiful expression of their personal faith in Christ, and often is witnessed by family and friends.

I also believe it is wise to accept the baptism by immersion of a believer that was baptized in another Bible teaching church. This demonstrates a respect for their faith and upholds the true meaning of baptism. It is insulting to someone to reject their baptism by immersion that took place in a Bible teaching church that instructed them on the correct mode, and the correct meaning. If they understood the meaning, then we should value their experience. Why place an unreasonable demand on solid believers that desire to join our fellowship?

Another area of respect that I try and demonstrate is in the area of Communion or the Lord's Supper. Before we partake of this sacred ordinance, I will take a moment and explain the various views. I will include a statement such as: "We certainly respect the various religious views concerning the Lord's Supper, but here at New Life we embrace the concept of the Memorial View."

Next, we invite anyone who believes in Christ to join us as we partake of the Lord's Supper. We leave the decision of participation to the individual conscience of each person attending the service. This practice of "open communion" is a beautiful picture of an approaching day in heaven when we all gather at the feet of Jesus. After all, there certainly will not be any denominational labels to separate us at the throne of God.

Closely related to the idea of religious respect is the important concept of demonstrating some cultural sensitivity. It is valuable to be sensitive to those who come to Christ from religious backgrounds that may see a few things a little *I think it is fair to say, that most of us read the Bible with "cultural eyes" to some extent.* differently. I think it is fair to say, that most of us read the Bible with "cultural eyes" to some extent.

For example, the little country church that I grew up in considered smoking a sinful behavior. In fact, your salvation might be "called into question" if you used tobacco in any way. This "sinful vice" was really "frowned upon" by the church. When the guest evangelist came to town for a spring or fall revival, he would address the subject with great clarity. Repentance was the "battle cry" from the pulpit for all smokers in the church! Believe me, smoking was not compatible with the Christian faith of that little country church of my childhood.

However, the attitude was much different in some sections of the country where tobacco was a common crop of the farmers. It did not bother the conscience of Christians that smoked because it was such a part of their economic structure. They might choose to quit for many reasons, but seldom did they stop smoking based on a need to repent of sin. Basically, smoking was an accepted behavior by churches in certain cultures.

This was also true with churches Beyond the Bible Belt that primarily consisted of southern transplants. For example, the First Southern Baptist Church of Mishawaka, IN, literally had a designated "smokers tree" near the church building. Every week, several members gathered by the tree, right after Sunday School for a cigarette. Then they went back inside to sing great hymns of the faith, and enjoy the preaching of God's Word. As soon as the Worship Service was over, they gathered once again by the "tree of fellowship" for another cigarette. It was an accepted practice of many of the charter members because they shared a similar cultural background. Therefore, it was not viewed as a *stumbling block that might offend a weaker brother* (Romans 14:21). It was simply an issue of personal choice based on the conscience of the individual.

Generally speaking, it is wise to give people a little "breathing room" in the area of Christian liberty. It is also healthy to try and understand someone by looking at an issue from their point of view. Listening to one another is a great place to start. It is also helpful to understand that it is not "liberal" to have Christian unity in the midst of cultural diversity. After all, that was a primary emphasis of the congregational meeting found in the fifteenth chapter of Acts.

Generally speaking, it is wise to give people a little "breathing room" in the area of Christian liberty.

At this juncture, I want to make an important observation. When many people came to America through Ellis Island, during the European Immigration, less than 2% settled in the south. Obviously, that means that 98% of the European immigrants settled in regions of our country Beyond the Bible Belt. Many of these folks represented more formal aspects of Christianity, such as found in the Lutheran and Catholic Faiths. Along with deep religious roots, many have a rich family cultural heritage as well.

Therefore, it is very important to demonstrate some religious respect, and cultural sensitivity as we minister Beyond the Bible

Belt. It is a huge step for people to take their faith from a formal religion to a personal relationship with Christ. As they take this giant leap of faith, they may not automatically abandon their cultural heritage. In fact, their celebrations may continue to resemble their cultural background.

For example, their wedding reception is considered a festive occasion that includes a full meal and friendly dancing. It may also include a beverage for the wedding toast that is slightly stronger than sparkling cider. Other family celebrations may include a glass of fine wine at special dinner, or a "frosty cold one" to "wash down" a slice of pizza. This has been deeply engrained in their family culture, and even their religious roots for many generations. Therefore, it is important not to "cast a judgmental rock" and carelessly insult their cultural heritage.

Do not get me wrong; I am not suggesting that we put a wine cellar in the church basement, or "roll out the barrel" at the next church picnic. I am simply trying to provide some helpful insight concerning some, who have come to Christ, from a completely different cultural background. After all, it may prove beneficial to "walk a mile in their shoes" in order to better understand their walk with God.

Before my fundamentalist friends throw this book into the fireplace and brand me a heretic, just consider for a moment the following question. What conclusions could be drawn from a casual reading of the Bible concerning Christian conduct? In other words, if someone reads the Bible without any preconceived ideas, is it possible that a different conclusion than yours could be arrived at? If so, give the person a break, and avoid judging their spirituality in a negative way.

It is also helpful to realize that some people from other cultures may even "question" some of our behavioral practices. For example, some believers in poverty stricken nations may consider the American Christian lifestyle as lavish and extravagant. They may struggle with the concept of a "conservative Christian" owning a big house, several suites of clothes, a car for every driver in the family, and taking expensive vacations, etc.

On the other hand, we recognize these abundant provisions as blessings from God. Therefore, we enjoy them with a heart of gratitude. My point is simply this: our values are influenced to some degree by our cultural backgrounds. Understanding this principle may help give others "a little grace" concerning the "cultural influence" on biblical interpretation, in the area of Christian conduct.

It really comes back to the principle of thinking like a missionary as discussed in a previous chapter. Most missionaries serving in European countries have learned to "tone down the rhetoric" on certain cultural practices that have been going on for centuries. This helps keep the people from "turning a deaf ear" to the message of the missionary.

It is a wise practice overseas, and in some areas of the United States, particularly beyond the Bible belt, it is just as wise to apply the same principle. Bottom line, a little religious respect, and cultural sensitivity, will go a long way in promoting the idea: *In the essentials unity, in the non-essentials liberty, and in all things charity.*

CHAPTER 18

ALL THE LONELY PEOPLE

The old Beatles song, Eleanor Rigby, included that classic line: "Look at all the lonely people." They described several common faces in the crowd of life, that all had one tragic theme, loneliness. Unfortunately, those words also describe the average congregation that gathers for worship on any given Sunday. Sometimes, behind the smiles, are lives filled with the pain of loneliness. Yes, many people who gather to worship the Lord, experience the feeling of being alone in a crowd of fellow believers.

There sits a husband and wife that buried their son who was killed in a tragic car accident. Across the aisle is a man that lost his wife to her battle with cancer. Also in the congregation, sits a woman, who suffers alone with the pain of her husband's secret lifestyle of infidelity. Near the back, sits a young man that suffers with the shame of his continual struggle with drug addiction. Another man battles his porn addiction, and his heart grows cold to spiritual things. Seated in the congregation is an adult woman that still lives with the emotional scars from being molested as a child. Also in the crowd is a person trying to seek refuge, while facing the reality of financial ruin. Parents that are battling with teenage rebellion, wonder if it will ever end? Other parents that have experienced the heartbreak of a son or daughter that walked away from the Lord, wonder where they went wrong? Another family recently learned that their son is gay, and they wonder how it could happen?

In our broken culture, it is essential that believers receive large doses of encouragement. According to Hebrews 10:25, it is a primary reason we gather to worship. Basically, encouragement is simply inspiring someone with hope. This is very important because when there is hope for the future, there is power in the present.

In our broken culture, it is essential that believers receive large doses of encouragement.

The Lord drove this truth deep in my heart when a 21-year old young man in our church was tragically killed in a car accident. My wife and I visited the grieving parents and listened to their sad, sad story. It seems that their son had become heavily involved in drugs. They had tried to help him for a few years. He even went to rehab for three months shortly before his tragic death. As we sat and listened to these grieving parents, our hearts ached for them. Their pain was so real and their sorrow was nearly overwhelming.

They are a wonderful Christian couple with a mature faith in the Lord. Unfortunately, they had been dealing with an all too common problem with their son. We sat and listened, and were once again reminded of the pain and suffering that people are experiencing in the privacy of their lives. We wept with them as they described the "bubbly personality" of their son.

He was a young man with a big smile. He "lit up a room" with his magnetic personality the moment he walked in. I had served as his pastor for several years and watched him grow up in the church. He was active in our Sunday School as a child, and regularly attended the Youth Group as teenager. He had a big smile and everyone loved him, yet behind the smile was a life of pain and addiction.

It broke our hearts as we listened to their story. We wrapped our arms around them and prayed for God's sustaining grace during their time of great sorrow.

When we got in our car to drive away, I turned to my wife and said, "It is time to develop a better support system in our church." We knew that we could not wait any longer to implement our vision of the "positive faith team" concept for uplifting relationships in the body of believers. The word TEAM forms an acrostic as follows:

Trusting one another.

Encouraging one another.

Accepting one another.

Ministering to one another.

Our goal is to provide a "grace gathering" of love and acceptance where people can open up and help each other. These "positive faith teams" are the basis for providing general encouragement and vast amounts of loving support for any problem. In a nutshell, our concept is to develop a positive atmosphere of faith, hope, and love. The Apostle Paul said in I Corinthians 13:13, *And now abide faith, hope, and love, these three; but the greatest of these is love.*

Jesus said in John 13:34-35: *A new commandment I give to you, that you love one another; as I have loved you, that you also love one another. By this all will know that you are My disciples, if you have love for one another.* The ultimate "badge of the believer" is our love for one another. Therefore, friendships rooted in unconditional love will embrace the core Christian values of mercy and grace

Consequently, creating a trusting environment is an important first step for developing a loving positive faith team. After all, trust is the foundation of all healthy relationships. People have to know that they can share their burdens, and expect them to remain confidential to the group. Therefore, trust is absolutely essential for a positive faith team to successfully "do the Christian life together."

Next, they need to be able to encourage one another with hope. People need large doses of loving encouragement to survive. Hope is a powerful force. It could be described as the momentum of life. We see this in football all the time. One team is trailing and it looks like the game is over. Then the other team causes a turnover. It may be a blocked punt, a recovered fumble, or an intercepted pass. You can almost write the script from there. The tidal wave of momentum begins to shift, and the final outcome is almost inevitable. The same is true in life. When hope is born in the heart, victory over the problems of life becomes a reality of positive faith.

The next aspect is to accept one another. An atmosphere of acceptance is absolutely crucial for people to open up and share *An attitude of acceptance* their problems. If people sense a *communicates an atmos-* condescending spirit or a judg- *phere of trust.* mental atmosphere of condemna- tion, they will simply keep their problems to themselves. Accepting one another will be vital for people to be vulnerable. An attitude of acceptance communicates an atmosphere of trust.

It says that you are safe here. We are not going to judge you or question your spiritual maturity simply because you have a prob- lem. It affirms the fact that people of genuine faith can have very real problems. It also sets the stage for people to seek the help they need.

An accepting spirit says that we understand that real Christians have real problems. This paves the way for an open and honest atmosphere of Christian love. It is taking Romans 8:1 at face value where the Scripture says: *There is now no condemnation to those who are in Christ Jesus.*

Do not get me wrong, accepting one another does not mean that we condone any and all actions of people. It simply means that we appreciate your honesty and we want to understand your problem. We are here for you and our desire is to *Bear one another's burdens, and so fulfill the law of Christ* (Galatians 6:2). It is the idea of unconditional love in action toward the people of faith, who simply need a fresh shot of hope. Therefore, developing an accepting atmosphere is crucial to avoid a condescending spirit of negative minded faith killers.

The final aspect of our positive faith teams is the concept of ministering to one another. This includes all types of ministry opportunities such as: providing meals during a time of need, hos- pital and nursing home visitation, hosting bridal showers and baby showers, retreats, and a wide variety of other ministry needs as determined by the individual positive faith teams. As we create an atmosphere of trust, encouragement, and acceptance, we set the stage to minister to one another.

In fact, the beauty of these positive faith teams is the natural opportunity to develop a team approach to ministry. Therefore, since every team needs a coach, leadership training is a big key to helping the positive faith teams be successful. Since everything rises and falls on leadership, we begin by looking for positive people to serve as leaders/facilitators. After all, it will be impossible to create a positive faith team with negative leaders. The five things we emphasize with the leaders are:

1. Embracing the mission of the Great Commission.
2. Embracing the local church as the God-given vehicle for discipleship.
3. Enthusiasm for the ministry of New Life.
4. Enthusiasm toward the concept of positive faith.
5. Enthusiasm for the value of unconditional love.

I have learned not to overlook the obvious. As I explained in a previous chapter, the Great Commission as revealed in Matthew 28:19-20 is one command that is surrounded by three participles. The single command is to *make disciples.* The process includes "going" (which implies winning people to Christ), "baptizing" (which implies identifying with Christ), and "teaching" (which implies instructing the believer in the Word of God in order to live for Christ). The leaders must understand and fully embrace our purpose, which is to make disciples.

The next step must be the embracing of the local church as the God-given vehicle for making disciples. It is crucial to understand that the local church is a "core value" of the New Testament. After all, 115 times the word for church *(ekklesia)* is used in the Greek New Testament. Only 23 times does it refer to the "universal church" and 92 times it refers to the "local church." This speaks volumes.

Do not get me wrong; we are not opposed to para-church organizations. However, the local church should be our passion as we follow the New Testament plan for making disciples. It has been my observation through the years that when Christians become more passionate about another Christian organization other than the local church, they become less effective in local church ministry. Therefore, it goes without saying that our positive faith team leaders need to be passionate about local church ministry.

The next aspect of importance is enthusiasm about the ministry of New Life. This really comes down to an issue of team chemistry. If leaders are excited about our ministry, it will create a contagious spirit of energetic momentum for the ministry. However, if they are unhappy with the direction of New Life, their group may become an anchor holding the ministry back, instead of an oar that is helping to row us forward. This can become a toxic situation and a pocket of poison. In that process we have to spend our time confronting leaders instead of cheering them on. Therefore, it is so much better for everyone if leaders are enthusiastic about the New Life ministry.

This leads to the importance of embracing the concept of positive faith. It is impossible to develop "positive faith teams" if negative people lead them! To embrace positive faith is to believe that the Word of God will bless your life. It is that simple.

The last thing I want to mention as a value for our positive faith team leaders is a heart of unconditional love. This is difficult to train, but easy to recognize because the cream naturally rises to the top. Basically, we look for people who love people. We want leaders who don't "shoot the wounded" nor practice "Christian cannibalism."

In other words, they look for a bandage to heal the hurting instead of a bayonet to stab them. They also do not engage in judgmental conversations about hurting people. They understand that real Christians can have real problems. Therefore, they would never dream of "kicking someone while they are down." Instead, they reach down in love with a helping hand to pick them up. This will enable people to open up and find the help they need from people who truly care about them.

Bottom line, a genuine "grace gathering" is a powerful way of helping people connect to the church through unconditional love and acceptance. As it has been so clearly stated in the theme song from "Cheers": "Sometimes you want to go where everybody knows your name, and they're always glad you came, troubles are all the same. You want to be where everybody knows your name." Perhaps, if the church grabbed this concept, the bars would be less packed, and the churches would be more packed. As we do a better job of encouraging all the lonely believers, it will also serve as a magnet for the gospel to unbelievers as well.

CHAPTER 19

WITH GOD IT IS
POSSIBLE TO OVERCOME OBSTACLES

The same battles will surface over and over again in a church seeking to build an effective Great Commission ministry. Well meaning people will become concerned that you are not "denominational enough" in your approach. Particularly the traditional believers who do not understand, (or sometimes don't even care) that you are trying to reach the community for Christ. Expect opposition when your goal is to build a hospital for the sinner, not a haven for the saint. Your ministry will comfort the afflicted, but it will also afflict the comfortable.

I suggest following the advice of Jesus: *Be wise as serpents and harmless as doves* (Matthew 10:16). A wise leader will not be naïve to the fact that some of the greatest opposition to a Great Commission ministry will be from the ranks of the saved. Believe me, those who oppose change can be ruthless. Make no mistake about it; they "play for keeps" and "take no prisoners."

Let me explain. Over the past several years we have transitioned from a handful of southern transplants to a congregation of several hundred people. As you know, much of our growth has come through evangelism. Our entire staff has also been developed from within our congregation. We are truly an indigenous church.

However, all through the years, there has been some form of resistance from some of the traditional denominationalist. The first one came from a man, who for the first seven years of my ministry, sat on the back row with his arms folded. For seven years (not weeks, nor months, but years) he stared, glared, and dared me to move him. Finally, when we relocated the church campus to our present location, he moved on.

Another attack on the ministry came from a denominational loyalist that moved in from another area. He tried to undermine the ministry and gained a small following in the process. He did not approve of clapping to songs, or applauding during our worship services. He felt our new believers were not "reverent" enough in their worship. He also strongly resisted changing the name of our church to better represent our ministry. However, after a few years the Lord moved him out of the way.

Next came a staff member that did not understand our mission. Basically, his cultural heritage blinded him from our community values. Eventually, the contention simply created too much conflict. It became counter-productive for our ministry, so we helped him become successful elsewhere. However, before he left the area, he "stirred the divisional waters" and attempted to gain a following. Fortunately, the Lord moved him on, and pruned our vine for a more fruitful ministry.

I will mention one more example. This complaint came from a well meaning, but "traditionally minded" member. In a lengthy private meeting, he shared his concerns with me in a very direct manner. Basically, it was another example of "traditional denominational thinking" raising its frustrated head. His complaints could be condensed into: removing "Baptist" from our name; our emphasis on positive faith; our style of music, and certain aspects of my leadership.

I politely told him: the "Baptist Banner" was not going to be waived; positive faith will remain our emphasis; the praise band would keep praising; and as Pastor, I would continue to lead to the best of my ability. Basically, it was made crystal clear that we were going to "stay the course" in our ministry focus.

I also pointed out to him that earlier in the same day, Chris, a very satisfied member, stopped by my office to let me know how much he loves the church. He understands the downplaying of "Baptist" in a Catholic community; he loves the concept of positive faith, enjoys our style of worship, and expressed his gratitude for my leadership. In fact, Chris had just turned down a significant promotion at the bank because he would have been required to move away. He said that his biggest reason for staying in the community was to keep his family at New Life!

My point is clear. You will never please everybody. Some will believe in the mission, and some will never understand it. There is *We all face opposition, but God's grace is sufficient.* a "price tag" for developing a Great Commission ministry. It is very challenging, but it is also very rewarding. It is important to remember that God is always on His throne. We all face opposition, but God's grace is sufficient. In fact, God can turn an adversity into an advantage, as He shapes our life to be more like Christ.

While we have faced some opposition, we have also seen God demonstrate His power to overcome opposition. The words: *With God all things are possible* (Matthew 19:26) have become a part of our DNA as a congregation. It has given us the faith to turn obstacles into opportunities to experience the power of God. It has literally changed the mindset of the people from a defeated spirit of doubt, to a conquering spirit of faith.

I could mention the faith of so many new converts, and positive church transfers that God has blessed us with through the years. Our ministry has been enriched with countless people that have "put their shoulder to the wheel" in the New Life ministry. However, I want to take this opportunity to honor two of my original prayer warriors, and three original deacons that have blessed this ministry for many years. From day one of my arrival at the church, they embraced the vision to reach our community for Christ.

There was Carrie, a senior saint and a tremendous woman of God. She prayed me into the church, and remained my faithful prayer warrior until God called her home. Carrie did not live to see our modern worship stadium with her eyes, but she dreamed of it in her prayers. New Life would not be where we are today without her prayers of faith.

There is also Mary, another senior saint and faithful prayer warrior. Many years ago, she told me that the devil would try to drive me out. However, she promised to pray for me daily because she believed I was "God's man" for the church. Her prayers have been a major factor in "defeating the devil" through the years.

Next there is Harold, one of the original five deacons when I came to the church. His heart for Great Commission ministry has been an incredible blessing to me as pastor. He and his wife Brenda have faithfully served the Lord for many years. Their happiness for the many people that have come to Christ is "written on their smiling faces."

Then there was James, another one of the original five deacons that helped call me as pastor. He stuck with the church through "thick and thin." He was an original charter member, and remained in the church until he went home to be with the Lord. He was faithful to the ministry and loyal to his pastor. James personally requested for me to preach his funeral. It was a privilege to honor the faith of one of the original "pillars" of the church.

Last, but certainly not least; I must mention Roy, a third member of the original five deacons that welcomed me as pastor. He has a "heart of gold" and is the most humble servant leader I have ever known. Roy and his wife Pat have cheerfully embraced every transition for the sake of the gospel. The blessing of God on our ministry is literally the fulfillment of their life-long dream. They love the Lord, and would not have missed this "gospel ride" for the world!

In fact, on September 21, 2008, we celebrated the 50-year anniversary of the first groundbreaking service of the original church. We had a tremendous service with several hundred in attendance, and we baptized eleven adults. At the conclusion of the service, New Life presented a plaque, with great appreciation, to Roy and Pat for their: *Many Faithful Years of Tremendous Service to the New Life Ministry, and For Being Outstanding Role Models of Positive Faith, Optimistic Hope, and Sacrificial Love.*

It was thrilling to see the church spontaneously give Roy and Pat a well-deserved thunderous standing ovation. As I watched the scene unfold, I reflected on my years of serving the Lord with Roy, this quiet hero of the faith. It was my privilege to honor his loyal commitment to Christ, and his dedication to reaching the lost.

Let me explain something very important to help you understand "the rest of the story" as the late Paul Harvey used to say. You see; Roy was the man who stood for the gospel many years ago, and stood up to his father, the original Patriarch of the church. Roy embraced the vision for the future, and broke with the tradition of the past. As pastor, I could not have a better friend than Roy. I have never forgotten his courageous stand for the gospel, which became one of the greatest defining moments in our ministry.

The Biblical statement: "With God all things are possible" is not a trivial phrase.

My friend, never under estimate what God can do through the power of His Word. The Biblical statement: *"With God all things are possible"* is not a trivial phrase. It is a powerful truth based on the promise of an all-powerful God. Believe it, and God will bless your life as you overcome every obstacle by faith.

CHAPTER 20

SWEET SATISFACTION

Proverbs 13:19 says: *A desire accomplished is sweet to the soul.* Sometimes, there is just something sweet concerning the way God brings things together. As a result, the Lord gives you an extra blessing for your labor of love. When this happens, drink deeply from the well of sweet satisfaction. The energy gained from God's "extra-measure of grace" will provide the strength for "another lap around the gospel track."

This has happened a number of times at New Life. However, one example that I want to share is from Easter Sunday in 2008. It was an extra-special day as God moved in a powerful way at New Life. We had been in our new worship stadium for 18 months, and converted the old auditorium into a first class recreational gym and Starbucks style coffee shop.

The energy gained from God's "extra-measure of grace" will provide the strength for "another lap around the gospel track."

The ministry was firing on all cylinders and the excitement was gaining tremendous momentum.

The church was packed. Our people had reached out in a concentrated way to invite their lost friends, and God blessed our collective efforts. The young children were attending "Promise Land" in our Positive Faith Gym, and our worship stadium was a "standing room only" crowd. Friends from all over the community had come to New Life as they searched for answers to life. They were from all walks of life, and a variety of religious backgrounds were represented as well. I could sense that God was about to do something very special. The Positive Faith Praise Band and Praise

Singers had led us in a dynamic worship experience, and they "set the table" for the Positive Faith Message.

I preached on the subject of Rescued by the Resurrection, and clearly presented the gospel message of good news concerning the death, burial, and resurrection of Christ for the sins of the entire human race. The Spirit of God was at work and people were "tuned in" to the message in a special way. I could see faces of despair coming to life from the message of faith, hope and love. At the close of the sermon, everyone was given the opportunity to trust in Christ as Savior and Lord. When I asked for a show of hands indicating their decision, hands were raised all over the building.

When we began to sing the closing song, the Spirit of God moved on many hearts in a special way. Without any high pressure at all, many people responded to a loving invitation to publicly affirm their private decision. Our trained counselors took people into a private prayer room to help them in their journey of faith. It literally looked like a miniature "Billy Graham Crusade" as people from all walks of life affirmed their faith in the Lord. It was a beautiful scene that I will cherish for a long, long time.

After the service, the New Life Staff and Ministry Team Leaders had the opportunity to personally welcome our guests in the coffee shop. We provided free smoothies for all ages, and specialty coffee drinks for adults as well. It was a great time to mix and mingle with our guests. It allowed us to get to know some people on a more personal level, which has been such a significant part of our ministry through the years.

As I drove home that day, my mind began to retrace just how far the Lord had brought us over the past several years. We had successfully transitioned a church, which once consisted of a small handful of southern transplants, into a vibrant congregation of several hundred people from our community. We had truly become an indigenous church.

I felt a deep sense of satisfaction and tremendous gratitude for the faithfulness of God. I slowly pondered the years of work that had culminated on this particular Sunday. God had affirmed "His hand" on the New Life Ministry many times before, but this day was extra-special. My heart burst forth in praise with this thought on my mind: To God be the glory, great things He has done!

My mind went back to that cold day in February of 1985 when I first dusted the snow off the sign of the old church. I was taking a class at Bethel College and the First Southern Baptist Church of Mishawaka, Indiana was right next to the college campus. Quite frankly, I thought the church was an abandoned building. It appeared as if the church had disbanded. However, I pulled my car off the side of the road and trudged through the snow to check out their sign. When I dusted the snow off the sign, I discovered their Service Times, but no name was listed as pastor. I decided to get to the bottom of this right away.

I visited the pastor of a Southern Baptist Church in South Bend, and he verified that the First Southern Baptist Church of Mishawaka was without a pastor. Fortunately, he took a liking to me right away, and suggested I give him my resume. He told me that he would pass along my resume to the church, and he was kind enough to include a cover letter of support as well. I was only 26 years old and had never served as a pastor of any church, so my resume was pretty thin to say the least. However, I knew that God had called me to preach, so I decided to "give it a shot" and see what the Lord would do.

I was soon given the opportunity to preach at the little church. The small attendance was probably best at the time because it limited the damage I could do with those early sermons! Actually, the congregation was responding in a positive way to the biblical preaching. In fact, they asked me to preach on a "pulpit supply basis" for the next few months. During this time, the church began to grow. Somehow word began to spread that a "new kid on the block" was preaching at First Southern.

It was exciting to see some sparks of life in a congregation that had dwindled through the years. The "culminated sign" that I was to serve as the next pastor came on a Sunday evening in May of 1985. A young couple came forward for membership. They told me that they liked my preaching and wanted to join the church. They shared that they wanted to raise their kids in a Bible teaching church, and liked the idea of me serving as their pastor. I thanked them for the gracious compliment, but informed the couple that I was not the pastor of the church. I was simply filling in while the church searched for their next pastor.

I guess this got the ball rolling because within a week, I was asked to candidate for the position as pastor. My wife and I prayed about it and we felt that God had brought us to the church for "such a time as this." We recognized the desperate need for an evangelistic, Bible teaching church in our Catholic community. Notre Dame University is only a "stone's throw away" and Catholicism has a significant influence on the community at large.

We knew the challenge would be great, but we also had great faith in God. We chose Matthew 19:26 as our foundational verse. Jesus said: *With men these things are impossible, but with God all things are possible.* Those hope filled words of Christ quickly became the strength of my life, and our theme for the New Life ministry.

Many years have transpired from the "early days" of ministry. The congregation has transitioned into a vibrant group of several hundred people, with much of the growth coming through evangelism. We have relocated the church campus, successfully completed three major building programs (including three and a half years of renting the Seventh Day Adventist Church during our first building program), and brought the influence of positive faith to the community.

Yes, as I drove home from church after God had moved so powerfully that Easter, there was a deep sense of fulfillment in my heart. The words of Proverbs 13:19 rang very true to me that day. The biblical concept of: *A desire accomplished is sweet to the soul*, was a living reality in my heart. I certainly experienced a rewarding feeling as I thought about the events of the day, and reflected on the years of labor in ministry. Once again, souls had come to

Christ, and I felt that "sweet satisfaction" in my soul for serving the Lord.

Now we conduct multiple services during the Easter weekend to accommodate the crowds. God continues to bless His Word beyond my wildest dreams. It is truly a sweet satisfaction to observe the life-changing power of the gospel. Yes, preaching the

It is truly a sweet satisfaction to observe the life-changing power of the gospel.

gospel brings a sweet satisfaction from the Lord. It is a tremendous joy to proclaim the good news of God's incredible love.

My friend, the New Life story in a nutshell, is simply the power of the gospel to transform lives. God took a little group of people struggling to keep their doors open, and impacted our community for Christ. If He can do that in towns like Mishawaka, and Osceola, Indiana; then He can do it in your town as well. Remember, you can go anywhere from nowhere! Therefore, stay faithful and stay thirsty, my friends. You will drink deeply from the well of sweet satisfaction.

ABOUT THE AUTHOR

Michael A. Cramer is the founder of the Power for Living Ministry, and Senior Pastor of New Life Church. His emphasis on positive faith encourages believers, and builds a bridge to those exploring the Christian faith. His inspirational style helps people relate to the timeless truth of scripture. His evangelist spirit helps people from all walks of life connect with Christ. Mike has a tremendous passion to help people develop the confidence to overcome obstacles, and achieve true success in life. He believes that any challenge can be conquered with the positive faith that embraces the powerful truth that "with God all things are possible." Mike impacts leaders in the faith, business, and athletic communities with his positive approach to Biblical preaching, motivational speaking, inspirational books and radio broadcast. His influence with leaders has expanded his ministry far beyond the borders of New Life. His greatest joy in life is the opportunity to minister at home. Mike and his wife, Cindi, have four grown children and three grandchildren.

OTHER BOOKS BY THE AUTHOR

Power Moments

Fifty-two short chapters that are easy to read, and filled with positive motivation and powerful inspiration. *Power Moments* captures the spirit of success from a Christian perspective. It is designed to inspire the human spirit and motivate winners in the game of life. It is an excellent book to uplift the believer with an encouraging message of hope. It is also a valuable resource for low-key evangelism.

Power Moments is also available in Spanish.

Dynamics of Effective Leadership Development

This book is a twelve-session Bible study on the foundational values for effective ministry. It is an outstanding resource for individual or group study.

Note: To secure your copy of any of the books by Michael A. Cramer, please follow the suggested donation structure listed in *Fireside Chats To Fire Up Churches*. Thank you.

CONFERENCE SCHEDULING

Michael A. Cramer is a gifted communicator and an effective leader. Mike is an experienced keynote speaker and offers valuable insight on: Leadership, Family Values, Evangelism, Biblical Instruction, and Positive Motivation.

You may contact Mike at:
Power for Living Ministry
P.O. Box 4396
South Bend, IN 46634
Email: pflmike@aol.com
www.nlpositivefaith.com

ORDER FORM

For each additional copy, please send the suggested donation of $15.00 to:

> Power for Living Ministry
> P.O. Box 4396
> South Bend, IN 46634
> Email: pflmike@aol.com
> www.nlpositivefaith.com

For bulk quantities, contact us for special arrangements.
All orders include the cost of shipping.

The purpose of the Power for Living Ministry is to communicate a positive Christian message and empower people to achieve success through the motivational and inspirational teaching of sacred truth.

Thank you for helping us share the positive faith that believes:

With God all things are possible.